CAPTAIN CAP
His Adventures, His Ideas,
His Drinks

OTHER TITLES BY ALPHONSE ALLAIS
PUBLISHED BY BLACK SCAT BOOKS

Masks
(2012)

How I Became an Idiot by Francisque Sarcey
(2013)

CAPTAIN CAP

HIS ADVENTURES, HIS IDEAS, HIS DRINKS

ALPHONSE ALLAIS

Translated and with an introduction, notes,
& illustrations by Doug Skinner

BLACK SCAT BOOKS

CAPTAIN CAP

His Adventures, His Ideas, His Drinks

by Alphonse Allais

Translated from the French by Doug Skinner

ACKNOWLEDGEMENTS:

Portions of this translation first appeared—in slightly different form—in four volumes of the *Absurdist Texts & Documents* series.

Chapter XXII appeared in *Black Scat Review* #5.

ISBN-13 978-0-615-84340-7

First Edition

Black Scat Books
BlackScatBooks.com

"Nobody in his entourage remembered him otherwise than half intoxicated or frankly drunk. In his conversation, emitted in a nasal tone, which gave it additional charm, boasting blossomed artlessly into incoherence... In Allais's hands, this sedentary lout became the hero of wild adventures. He assumed their paternity with false modesty and secret pride. So much so, that Allais once told me, 'It's come to the point where I don't know if I'm making fun of him, or he's making fun of me!'"

—Hugues Delorme

CONTENTS

A Few Words About Captain Cap

Many discerning readers think Alphonse Allais was the finest humorist France ever produced. I will have to concur. Many class him simply as a master of the short story. I will have to agree with that as well. And many claim that his greatest creation was that hard-drinking adventurer and inventor, Captain Cap. I will go along with that too, but with one quibble: as you will soon see, Captain Cap really existed.

But first a brief bio of Allais himself is in order, since he's not well known to English readers. He was born October 20, 1854, in Honfleur, a northern port town: the same day as Rimbaud, and in the same town as Satie. His father was a pharmacist; and so Alphonse dutifully went to Paris to study for the family business. Paris, however, held other attractions, and he soon discovered the cafes and cabarets of Montmartre, where he partied with Hydropathes, Fumistes, and other bohemians. He began writing monologues for cabarets, and then comic essays for journals. Eventually, he abandoned pharmacy, and devoted his life to coming up with a column three or four times a week. He first appeared in Montmartre papers like *Le Chat Noir* and *Tintamarre*; later, better paying ones, like *Le Journal* and *Le Sourire*.

His column, usually under his preferred rubric *La Vie Drôle (The Funny Life),* was unpredictable: stories, fables, dialogues, inventions, real and fake letters. It was sometimes violent, scatological, and anticlerical. According to legend, he always wrote in a cafe, at the last minute, and mailed off the piece without rereading it. This is not exactly true, but not exactly false, either. Rather than rewrite a clumsy sentence, he would comment on it, or pass it off as a quotation. When inspiration flagged, he resorted to transparent padding, repetition, running jokes, quotations, misquotations, and catch phrases.

He sometimes informed the reader how much space he had left to fill. As he once put it, "It doesn't matter if I write one thing instead of another, since it's just to kill time. (As if, poor fool that I am, it is not time that kills us.)"

Particularly in his later pieces, he was intrigued with recreational linguistics: puns, eye rhymes, syllable rebuses (like the English "N M E" for "enemy"). He had a penchant for the "fable-express," a verse fable with a punning moral, and the "holorime," in which two lines of verse are homonyms. We also owe him the creation of the "neo-alexandrine," in which unequal lines averaged twelve syllables—and in which only the first words rhymed.

The columns seem to have satisfied his literary ambition. They were collected in annual volumes, with titles like *Two and Two Is Five, The Squadron's Umbrella, Pink and Apple-Green.* He collaborated on a few plays, none particularly successful; he salvaged one by turning it into a novel *(The Badger Affair).* In 1883 and 1884, he exhibited several monochromatic canvases (with titles like "First communion of anemic girls in a snowstorm"), a silent funeral march ("for the greatest sorrows are mute"), and a baked potato (since *"pomme de terre cuite"* also means "terra cotta apple") at the *Salon des Incohérents.* He married a woman named Marguerite Gonzée; apparently the marriage was unhappy. He was, according to friends, morose, lazy, and mischievous.

Unlike many writers, his background was not in literature. Although he was a remarkably poor student, his training in chemistry set him apart from the poets who filled Montmartre. It became part of his persona: when the caricaturist Cabriol depicted him on the cover of *L'Hydropathe* (January 28, 1880), it was as a pharmacist, mixing up stories with a mortar and pestle.

Allais cultivated the image himself in *Le Chat Noir* (January 6, 1882): "Alphonse Allais, masculine meridional, born in Pézenas; agricultural pharmacist, bottle inspector at the Invalides, knight of three distinguished orders; ex-dentist for three crowned heads, Alphonse Allais, the blond ephebe, chased by scandal from a peaceful pharmacy..." He proclaimed himself on the "science faculty of the Chat Noir," and contributed sprightly doggerel about chemical reactions:

"The density of oxygen
Is calculated nicely,
At 1.1056, when
You put it most precisely..."

And the pharmacy itself often provided inspiration, as in the early story "Comfort": unable to find a urinal after a night of carousing, he heads for a pharmacy, where he asks to leave a urine sample to be tested for diabetes.

Throughout his later career, he maintained a vivid interest in scientific discoveries, with many columns inspired by specialists' journals. Humorists have often waxed nostalgic or sentimental; Allais was resolutely progressive—with the added fillip that his proposals were ridiculous. Nevertheless, he coolly provided precise technical details, including chemical formulas.

He did, incidentally, work in the laboratory throughout his life. He was issued a patent in 1881 for a sweetened instant coffee for soldiers, inspired by his own military service. With his brother Paul, he worked on color photography; with Charles Cros—another scientifically minded bohemian—on synthetic rubber. Many of the inventions that he and Cap discuss in the following stories, however, probably never made it to a prototype.

And Captain Cap? He did really exist, although he often seemed to put little effort into it. His real name was Albert Jean Baptiste Nicolas Caperon, and he was born in Paris in 1864. His father, Paulin Caperon, had inherited a fortune in his twenties, and devoted himself to radical politics, bibliomania, and banking, in no particular order. It was while practicing the last that he sold railway shares in Alsace to a Swiss bank; when Germany annexed Alsace in 1871 after the Franco-Prussian war, Germany confiscated the stock. The Swiss bank wanted its money back, leaving Caperon in an uncomfortable situation. He resolved it by fleeing to Belgium, and then to America, where he adopted the name of Peter Coutts, and bought land in Mayfield, California (now Palo Alto).

He turned the property into a formidable dairy farm, with cattle imported from France. He built a brick tower for his library, and a cottage for his family: his wife Élisa, his daughter Marguerite, and young Albert. After six years, however, he returned to France to settle his affairs, selling the property to Leland Stanford, who later founded Stanford University. The cottage where the future Captain Cap grappled with adolescence now houses married Stanford students; the tower, now known as "Frenchman's Tower," is the subject of much local folklore.

The Caperons eventually resettled in Paris, where Paulin died in 1889. Albert was then 26. Like his father, he came into money at an early age; unlike him, he squandered it on cocktails. He married the niece of his childhood nanny, had two daughters, and played bit parts in a couple of amateur plays. Other than that, he was apparently blissfully idle.

Except, of course, for his tumultuous campaign for parliament in 1893, the subject of the first part of the book that follows.

Allais met Caperon at the Gardenia, a social and theatrical club founded by Paul Fabre, son of the Canadian high commissioner, and frequented by both Chat Noir regulars and Canadian ex-pats. Captain Cap, as he was already known, distinguished himself by accomplishing nothing and drinking heavily, and was heartily mocked by the Gardenians. Apparently he gave as well as he got: Allais confessed that he was never sure if he or Cap made more fun of the other. The Captain had a lively imagination and an American accent, both of which he exploited for his amusement. In the words of another admirer, the artist George Auriol, "He was a prodigious character... the only man to justify the meaning of the word aperitif: with every cocktail that he drank, he opened up more. He was as full of faults as you or I; but compared to ours, which are pale and dim, each of his was a pure diamond."

He became a frequent character in Allais's stories, a useful mouthpiece for all tall tales and curious inventions. According to contemporaries, Cap was given to boasting and flights of fancy, so perhaps he also supplied ideas. At any rate, he was an ideal foil for Allais, his truculence the perfect contrast to Allais's insouciance.

Alcohol, as you may notice, plays a crucial part in these stories.

Caperon was often described as always drunk. Allais was more often characterized as "between two drinks," neither drunk nor sober. They were both fond of the American and English bars that opened in Paris in the '90s. Occasionally (in the stories at least) Allais and Cap would swear off American cocktails as "coffin varnish," and return to wholesome French refreshments, but these resolutions were always fleeting.

Albert Caperon died in 1898, after a fall from a horse. He was only 34. He subsequently disappeared from Allais's columns.

Dorothy Parker once remarked that most humorists "milk a formula until it moos in pain." After years of turning in columns, Allais may have been feeling the strain. In a series of rather glum installments in 1901 (July 25, July 31, August 9), he simply listed recent patent applications. Contemplating such genuine inventions as the luminous hat, the pedal-operated fan, the combination fishing pole and bicycle pump, the hail parasol, the gloves made from intestinal membranes, the multicolored cane, the sea soap, the summer fez, the metal legs for wooden horses, "etc., etc., etc.," he could only remark, "Fantasists who think they're so clever when they imagine dust-catchers for submarines, or rubber muzzles to prevent snails from dribbling on the salad, are small beer beside certain serious and licensed inventors." Fact, all too often, trumps fiction, to the eternal despair of humorists.

Perhaps that was what led him to turn to earlier inspiration, and to revive Captain Cap. Perhaps, too, he was nostalgic for his Bohemian youth; he never really took to marriage and respectability. In his column for May 23, 1901, he recalled "that poor Captain Cap," and announced a new collection: "Speaking of Captain Cap, let us announce the upcoming appearance, published by Juven, of *Captain Cap, His Life, His Work, and What Remains to Be Accomplished of His Program,* by Mr. Alphonse Allais, cover and preface by Mr. George Auriol, table of contents by Mr. Armand Berthez." Auriol and Berthez were old friends of both Allais and Cap, but the volume eventually appeared without them.

With the revised title *Captain Cap: His Adventures, His Ideas, His Drinks,* it appeared in 1902. It contained the Captain Cap stories Allais had written over the years, a dossier on Cap's political spree, and an appendix of his favorite cocktails. Allais didn't have enough

Cap material to fill a book, so he inserted Cap into some of his recent columns and earlier stories.

It was to be Allais's last book. There's a bit of a valedictory tone to it; the footnotes are often nostalgic, and the repeated "How long ago it was!" not entirely facetious. He continued to write several columns a week, for *Le Journal* and *Le Sourire,* until his death in 1905, at the age of 51. He was increasingly forgetful, drank too much, racked up debt, and put on weight; his marriage crumbled. The last years were marked by a slow decline.

But *Captain Cap* lived on. It remained in print, with a variety of imaginary Cap portraits gracing the covers of successive editions. The first translation that I know of was into Czech, by one Jindřich Hořejší, in 1923. Fittingly, he also translated Jaroslav Hašek's *The Good Soldier Švejk* into French; he was apparently fond of hard-drinking tricksters. Enrico Piceni translated Cap into Italian in 1930, as well as Allais's novel and a collection of short stories. Juan Esteban Fassio, the founder of the *Instituto de Altos Estudios Patafísicos de Buenos Aires,* frequented by such *porteño* celebrities as Borges and Cortázar, transmuted Cap into fine Argentine Castilian in 1972. The next year, Franco de Sousa brought out a Portuguese edition, about which I have no interesting tidbits, I'm afraid.

There has even been a sequel. In 1991, André Grall, a member of the distinguished A3 *(Académie Alphonse Allais)*, published *Le Retour du Captain Cap; le joyeux compère d'Alphonse Allais (The Return of Captain Cap: Alphonse Allais's Merry Sidekick).* The good Captain is reanimated to take on politics, AIDS, soccer, German reunification, the press, movies, war, religion, and other updated topics. (Parenthetically, I must confess I haven't read it; I'm quoting the blurb.) His fellow A3 members awarded him the Prix Alphonse Allais in 1992, so they must have liked it.

Given its wide and enduring popularity, why has there been no English translation until now? Heaven knows; but now there is.

There are, inevitably, topical references and quotations. I've decided to leave them intact, since the local color of *La Belle Époque* is enjoyably colorful; I've provided explanatory notes. The footnotes in the text are Allais's. The present work was originally published as four booklets by Black Scat Books, in February, April, August, and September, 2013; the demarcations have been kept in this edition, for reader comfort. We've also added eight Captain Cap stories that Allais published elsewhere, and a "Cappendix" of historical pictures. I am, let me add, indebted to the work of François Caradec, particularly his edition of Allais's complete work (La Table Ronde, 1964-1970) and his authoritative biography of Allais (Belfond, 1994).

Bon voyage, Captain Cap!

Doug Skinner
New York City
September, 2013

PART ONE
Captain Cap Before the Electorate

Captain Cap Before the Electorate

First of all, we must dispel one of the grossest errors of our time, and one of the most invidious.

"Captain Cap never existed," people state nowadays, in the bosoms of certain circles usually better informed.

What do they know, these people?

I acknowledge that you affirm the existence of someone when you know him, this someone, and when, trusting your senses, have seen, smelled, squeezed, and heard him.

And still remained on guard against hallucinations.

But, although the vicissitudes of life may have never put you in physical contact with an individual, to claim and to conclude that the individual does not or cannot exist—that takes the theories of the late Saint Thomas a bit too far.

It is the logic of the gentleman who said to the judge: "Three witnesses swear they saw me commit the theft. But I will name fifteen thousand who didn't!"

Let us not press the matter. Captain Cap, then, really existed. He was a charming man, and the following pages will have much to say about his character, his ideas, and his life.

And, furthermore, so that there remain no doubt on the real existence of our hero, we open this collection with several documents of indisputable authority: 1, his admirable proclamations to the citizens of the 2nd district of the 9th arrondissement, in which he sought their votes during the legislative elections of August 20, 1893; 2, the accounts of several rallies in which he presented and defended his platform; 3, appreciations of Cap's personality and original ideas from certain newspapers of the period.

Can there still be any doubt?

CITY OF PARIS
to the voters of the 9th arrondissement, 2nd district[1]
A WORD ABOUT CAPTAIN CAP

If you want to meet the man of the hour, look no further than in the skin of Captain Cap, your candidate.

Captain Cap! Everyone talks about him now, but how few really know him!

I have the honor of belonging to that small elite.

The first time I had the pleasure of meeting Cap was in the bar of the Hotel St. Petersburg; the second time in the Irish Bar on Royale Street; the third, in the Silver Grill; the fourth, in the Scotch Tavern; the fifth, in the Australian Wine Store on Eylau Avenue.[2]

I may have inverted the order of the bars, but, as they say in mathematics, the sum is still the same.

I liked Cap immediately. The stories of his adventures, the little exotic tunes that he liked to hum from time to time, his always novel observations, his hatred of bureaucracy and Europe: everything about Cap enchanted me, and we soon became excellent friends.

One can only profit from the company of such men, and the ideas that I acquired during my association with Cap verge on the prodigious.

Captain Cap has traveled extensively. When he says, "I spent three quarters of my life at sea, and two thirds of my existence on virgin land, etc., etc.," you must not see exaggeration, or bluffing, in this statement.

In Quebec, Cap performed for eighteen months the important duties of a starter at the Observatory.

It was he who launched the shooting stars.

In Labrador, Cap discovered the important cold cut mine ("Meat-Land") which are now the country's fortune.

I revealed, in a number of newspapers, close to a year ago, the absolutely plausible explanation for the existence of these nutritive quarries. I awaited refutations; none came.[3]

Our friend Cap, then, is a candidate for Parliament; I am familiar with the 2nd district of the 9th arrondissement, and I am tranquil.

That Cap win on the first ballot, I dare not affirm; but the second may well reserve some bitter disappointments for Mr. Strauss and Mr. Berger.[4]

Cap's platform is quite simple, and requires no explanation: he is anti-European and antibureaucratic.

Beyond these two great principles, all of the voter's demands are Cap's demands.

At the last rally, which was held in the Auberge du Clou, someone asked that Montmartre be leveled; Cap vowed to level Montmartre.

Cap also promised to prolong Trudaine Avenue to the Place de la Concorde.

"At which end?" inquired several voters.

"At both ends," replied the Captain.

A dramatic artist having interrogated the Captain on the question of greasepaint, which is, apparently, quite expensive, Cap promised to remove the tariff on German greasepaint, and even to promote its manufacture in France, on the model of the state factories in Sèvres and des Gobelins.

Captain Cap is not indifferent to the greasepaint question, for he has taken a great interest, and still takes a great interest, in the theater.

Recently, he created an important role in a play given at the Gardenia Society, and grandpa Sarcey did not hesitate to devote a flattering article to him on the front page of the Chat Noir.

It is now up to the universal franchise. We will know, Sunday evening, if Ledru and Rollin were right to fight so bitterly for this institution.

In one of Cap's proclamations, already familiar to you, we find this phrase, which we would do well to contemplate:

Far from being the privilege of a few, the pork barrel must become the privilege of all.

The man who spoke these words has a place with his name on it in the Palais-Bourbon.

Voters, to the polls, and no abstentions!

Vote for Captain Cap!

Hip! Hip! Hip! Hurray!

For a group of voters,

Signed: ALPHONSE ALLAIS

Approved by the candidate, Albert Caperon,

known as Captain Cap.

Captain Cap's Profession of Faith

Citizens:

A new man, I arrive with new ideas.

I want you to profit from these ideas, and that is why I come before you.

If you choose me, it is an honest man that you send to the Palais-Bourbon. I believe that I need say no more.

After twenty years at sea and in the Far West, when I set my foot again on my beloved native soil, what did I find?

Falsehood, calumny, hypocrisy, embezzlement, treachery, nepotism, extortion, fraud, and incompetence.

For the origin of these evils, citizens, look no further: it is the microbe of bureaucracy. And you do not negotiate with microbes.

YOU KILL THEM!

And that is what I have sworn to do, in spite of everyone.

Certain politicians, as you know, have an interest in maintaining this sorry state of affairs. They thrive and grow fat on the ruin of the people.

And they are already fat enough, these wicked men.

Let us drive them from us.

Far from being the privilege of a few, the PORK BARREL must become the privilege of ALL.

Let us then raise the alarm while there is still time.

The ship that we board is made of oak from the oldest forests of France. The sap of Gallic soil circulates in its flanks. If it leaks, let us patch it and keep an eye toward the bow.

Let us dump onto a desert island all of the dressed-up nullities who block us as we march forward.

Let us throw overboard all paperwork and registers, and make life-buoys from the chair cushions of these incompetents.

I have said what I wanted to say.

ENOUGH TALK!

We must clear ground before we sow. Let us clear ground!

When we have swept away the last speck of chaff, we will see blossom with ever greater brilliance *loyalty* and *love of country,* those two symbolic flowers without which the three words engraved on our buildings are in vain: *Liberty, Equality, Fraternity.*

Citizens,

You need a man of action; I am ready.

Until Sunday, then, and no abstentions.

Long live the Republic, free and without offices!

Albert Caperon, known as CAPTAIN CAP

Captain Cap's Platform

1. Establishment of a fort on Montmartre;
2. Establishment of an observatory on the same hill;
3. Place Pigalle a seaport;
4. Manufacture of greasepaint in France;
5. Abolition of the tax on bicycles;
6. Reestablishment of licentiousness on the street for the sake of repopulation;
7. Continuation of Trudaine Avenue to the great boulevards;
8. Abolition of bureaucracy;
9. Establishment of a bullfight arena and boat races on Montmartre;
10. Abolition of the School of Fine Arts, etc. etc.

Proclamation of a Group of VOTERS

Legislative election of August 23, 1893.
(9th arrondissement, 2nd district.)
Antibureaucratic and anti-European
committee.

Citizens:

Saint-Just said: "You overturned the aristocracy, but created the bureaucracy."

We have had a hundred years of this, and today the bureaucracy is more powerful than ever.

It has included everything, absorbed everything, invaded everything. It is what smothers geniuses and kills great ideas; it is the bleeding wound of Europe and the barrier to all progress.

Until now, no candidate who has presented himself has even suspected the existence of this formidable monster squatting at the doors of civilization.

This octopus with 100,000 tentacles, none has dared attack.

Now, one man has arisen:

CAPTAIN CAP.

And it is in the neighborhood of Saint-Georges that he has chosen to become the Saint George to this dragon.

A man arose, citizens, and this man looked around him.

His gaze was obscured by clouds of varnish.

Around him he saw nothing but paperwork, ignorance, carelessness, and routine.

"No more chair cushions," he cried. "For too long we have obeyed the blotters."

The time has come to overturn this Bastille of green cardboard.

And so, without hesitation, at our call, he abandoned everything, his ship and his cherished studies, to seize the wheel of the steamer of our demands.

"Everyone on deck," he commanded, "and board the bureaucratic galley."

Citizens, this is the man for you. We are as sure of him as we are of ourselves: we have his past as a guarantee. A distinguished astronomer, chemist, whaler, engineer, pearl diver, trapper, trader, and, above all, courageous mariner, he has, during his voyages around the globe, acquired incontestable experience.

Having kept in his heart a fierce love for his native land, he has conceived an implacable hatred for its worm-eaten institutions.

In the Far West, Captain Cap fought the Arapahoes. He defeated them; he scalped their chief.

He now wants to attack those who, in his vivid language, he calls the white savages, the most dangerous of all.

This, fellow citizens, is the grand outline of our platform.

The Captain, as he has told us, is dogmatically anti-European.

The expression of such a noble sentiment beggars all commentary.

So, citizens, to the polls, and no abstentions.

VOTE FOR ALBERT CAPERON
known as
CAPTAIN CAP

Maurice O'Reilly, Paul Frény, Alphonse Allais, Raoul Ponchon, George Auriol, Léon Gandillot, Howard Symonds, Georges Courteline, Emile Goudeau, Armand Berthez, Raphael Shoomard, Jean Prairial, Narcisse Lebeau, Paul Clerget, Henri Joseph, Prince Joe Masson, Barral, Brunais, Duplay, Gatget, Lacault, A. Bert, Jules Jouy, Gérault du "Cantal," Edouard Million, J. Paulet, Darcey, Alfred-Amand Montel, Jehan Sarrazin, Félix Huguenet, Paul Robert, Berthier.

A Campaign Rally For
CAPTAIN CAP

The evening began at 9:30.

It was led by citizen Maurice O'Reilly, who needs no introduction, and for whom the voters of the 9th arrondissement have many times expressed their appreciation.

The title of honorary president was bestowed on the exiled Alphonse Allais, victim of the infamous bureaucracy.[5]

After expounding Captain Cap's ideas in a few brief, but energetic, phrases, citizen Maurice O'Reilly read three telegrams that had just arrived:

(Saint-Malo) To you with all my heart and in spite of everyone. Alphonse Allais.

Raise a toast to Captain Cap, and drink to his success. Raoul Ponchon.

(Le Havre) Friends in le Havre, gathered at the cafe Régis, request us to send best wishes to the valiant Captain Cap, and cry three hurrahs in his honor. Fraternally yours, Jules Heuzet, Albert René, Vallette, Siegfried, Fautrel.

Captain Cap arose, visibly moved, declared himself extremely touched by these expressions of sympathy, and ended by saying that we would soon see whether he deserves them.

Citizen Berthez then took the floor with these words:

Citizens,

I have long known Captain Cap, I have followed him in many of his exploits; I even had the good fortune to accompany him on one of his voyages: I was therefore able to appraise him better than anyone, and that, citizens, is why I ask to speak.

Albert Caperon, better known as "Captain Cap," has reason to be proud of the title, for he earned it at the risk of his life, endangered a thousand times.

Citizens, I will attempt to retrace for you the different phases of his tormented life.

It is a heavy burden that I assume, given the few oratorical means at my disposal, but I am certain that you will listen with indulgence to the tale that I propose to tell.

Captain Cap, imbued since earliest childhood with the principles of democracy, was what is known as a precocious child, or more commonly an "infant prodigy," as was often remarked by an old friend of the family, since dead of a ruptured vessel which, I note in passing, clearly shows the importance of navigation in Captain Cap's surroundings.

Despite the comfortable position of his family, Captain Cap chose to sit on the benches of the parochial school.

He developed his theories on bureaucracy early...

At the age of ten, he posted a manifesto on the school walls, which would have led to his expulsion, had he not, by a discourse replete with philosophy, quickly rehabilitated himself in the eyes of his professors, who declared that they had never before encountered such an intellectual phenomenon.

At this already distant time, Captain Cap was not just another face in the crowd. And then (as now), it would have been childish or dishonest to deny it. (*Applause.*)

I continue. As Captain Cap advances in age, we see him triumphing in our schools, energetically defending his principles, and attracting proselytes.

Finally, at eighteen, nauseated by our relentless routine, and tired of vainly battling the incorrigible spirit of European bureaucracy, he heads for America.

There, my fellow citizens, a new life begins for the Captain; and, if I were permitted to take an oath here, on my own head, I could not find one strong enough to tell you, that without the knowledge that he possesses, and the unchecked energy that characterizes him, we might not have the joy of presenting him for your votes today. (*Hear, hear!*)

I will not enumerate all of Captain Cap's exploits, his life in the Far West and in Australia, his thousands of adventures at sea, his scientific work... no, that would take too long. Besides, others will tell it better than I could, in the time that I have available.

He lands in America with sixty francs; sets bravely to work in a shipyard, and, thanks to his intelligence, composure, and perspicacity, triumphing over all obstacles and accomplishing all the tasks confided to him, finally wins his title of Captain.

Later, having acquired a farm in California, he quarrels with the Indians. But Cap is a first-class horseman, a surer rifleman than the terrible Redskin, and none brandishes the bowie knife better than he; in eight days, he scalps three Indian chiefs, and puts his aggressors to flight.

I have mentioned the Captain's incomparable composure. A simple anecdote by illustration:

A train with 200 passengers (among them Captain Cap), was descending a steep hill on one of the largest lines in America, when suddenly the brake shattered, despite the desperate efforts of the engineer.

The train began to roll downhill at a vertiginous speed. Cries racked the air, and the panic was such that most of the passengers threw themselves onto the track, and were reduced to smithereens.

When, twenty-two hours later, the train finally came to a halt, Captain Cap was found calmly seated on a sack of corn, smoking his pipe and reading a back issue of the *Herald*...

I think, citizens, that such exploits require no comment. (*Yes, yes, bravo!!!*)

If I tell you these things, citizens, if I tell you these stupefying things, and if I add that a few years later, having lost his ship and cargo in the Arctic seas, Captain Cap rescued his crew, discouraged and decimated by scurvy, and if I quickly list some of the Captain's adventures, believe me, it is not to astonish you. It is simply to show you that this man, at once mariner, scholar, and philanthropist, will valiantly steer the ship whose wheel you have resolved to confide to him.

This is the man that I present to you. Judge him, and question him.

For my part, I step down, convinced that he has earned your support. (*Frenetic applause.*)

After citizen Paul Frény listed Captain Cap's artistic accomplishments, and demonstrated in a few words the advantage of such a representative for an artists' quarter, Captain Cap answered with clarity and precision different questions from citizens Quinel, Georges Albert, Brandimbourg, etc.

Citizen Howard Symonds asked the Captain in English about the anti-European question.

The Captain replied that he is, in spite of everything, a child of old Europe, a Parisian and a Frenchman. What he wants to fight and to abolish is dull routine, and the bureaucratic ideas that are the shame of Europe. (*Loud applause greeted these words.*)

Citizen Brunais questioned the Captain on the subject of hot water fountains.

The Captain replied in these words:

"I am not, for the moment at least, in favor of hot water fountains, given that I want to represent the people, not to delude them. It is proposed that we establish hot water fountains for people who have no homes, and who, living in shacks, have few possessions. Hot water would be useless to them when they have no place to put it. Before dazzling the people by promising them hot water, we must furnish them with receptacles to contain it." (*Hear, hear! Unanimous applause.*)

At 11:30, citizen Maurice O'Reilly adjourned the meeting. A crowd gathered on Trudaine Avenue, and three cheers were raised for the Captain as he regained his carriage.

The enthusiasm reached such a height that the horse was unhitched, and the voters pulled the Captain's carriage for twenty meters.

But Captain Cap slips away from ovations.

In less time than it takes to write, he jumped into another cab, and lifting his hat, disappeared, crying:

"No more bureaucracy! No more European routine! No more white savages!"

The secretary of the Committee,
Signed, George Auriol.

The PRESS and CAPTAIN CAP

The campaign of Captain Cap, the anti-European and antibureau-cratic candidate, is taking an excellent turn in the 9th arrondissement, 2nd district.

A membership and publicity committee has already formed. We call attention to the fine names of Alphonse Allais, Courteline, Gandillot, Ponchon, Emile Goudeau, Narcisse Lebeau, Paul Clerget, Prince Joe Masson, Jules Jouy, Gérault (du Cantal), Jehan Sarrazin, Félix Huguenet, Paul Robert, Berthier. (*L'Echo de Paris*, August 11, 1893.)

The illustrious Captain Cap, who has been in the papers so much recently, stands for office as an anti-European and antibureaucratic candidate.

Captain Cap is a new man, with big ideas, a declared enemy of routine and paperwork.

We hope that he will be elected. (*Le Diable au corps*, Brussels, August 7, 1893.)

A new candidate has just emerged in the 9th arrondissement of Paris who deserves a mention, for his platform departs from the usual banality.

The new candidate is Mr. Caperon, or "Captain Cap."

He proclaims himself antibureaucratic and anti-European. If he expounds his platform, especially the second part, in a public meet-ing, his listeners will not be bored. (*Le Petit Journal*, August 7, 1893.)

An enormous crowd, estimated at several hundred voters from the 9th arrondissement, and other arrondissements as well, packed one of the rooms of the Auberge du Clou last night to hear Captain Cap's profession of faith.

The meeting was very lively. The doors were broken down by several young ladies whose cards were anything but electoral. We note with regret that the candidate expressed no desire in his platform for women's suffrage. The election of the committee sparked numerous protests, the candidate having declared himself against committees.

Finally, citizen Captain Cap's candidacy was acclaimed unanimously, minus three votes. (*L'Echo de Paris,* August 13, 1893.)

Montmartre will always be Montmartre. Every night, in the Auberge du Clou, they acclaim the candidacy of Captain Cap, supported by the finest flower of the local humorists, Alphonse Allais, Courteline, the painter Robert, etc.

The issues that the honorable Captain Cap promises to champion are:

Lifting Paris to the height of Montmartre; forbidding the disposal of unlit tunnels on the public thoroughfare; creation of a Fort-Observatory on Montmartre, where the telescopes would serve as cannons; creation of a Council on signals to punish railway accidents; etc., etc. (*Le Figaro,* August 16, 1893.)

THE ELECTIONS
Paris - 9th arrondissement - 2nd district

The voters of the 2nd district of the 9th arrondissement met on August 6 at the Auberge du Clou, and, after having heard citizens O'Reilly, Berthez, Georges Albert, Paul Frény, Quinel, Brunais, etc., etc, and the frank and energetic declarations of Captain Cap, acclaim his candidacy unanimously, except for three votes, and will work towards his victory on August 20.

CAPTAIN CAP

We cannot claim to introduce to you the celebrated Captain Cap, as you are already familiar with his joyful anti-European and antibureaucratic campaign, led under the auspices of Allais and Courteline. We would have liked to meet with him, and learn what he thinks of his 176 votes; but, like all other candidates, despite his fraternal assurances, he no sooner collected the votes of his electorate than he forgot and abandoned them—the ingrate! At the Auberge du Clou where he regularly held his rallies, we were told that he had not been seen for four days. His printer told us where the socialist candidate usually takes his meals. There, we learned that Captain Cap has left for Normandy to restore himself after the tiring campaign... (*L'Eclair*, August 28, 1893.)

It is only for the record that we recall the orgy of colorful posters, some exaggeratedly laudatory, others viciously defamatory, that covered the walls of Paris this morning, and which constituted, to use the political jargon, the last desperate efforts. It is the whimsical candidates who win the prize in this Homeric battle of little flyers against giant broadsheets.

In Montmartre, Captain Cap, a humorist, born no doubt under the sails of the Moulin de la Galette, has flooded his district with proclamations such as these:

"After twenty years at sea, what do I find on my return to my country? Hatred, hypocrisy, embezzlement, nepotism, incompetence...

"For the origin of these evils, citizens, look no further: it is the microbe of bureaucracy. And you do not negotiate with microbes.

"YOU KILL THEM!" (*Le Matin,* August 21, 1893.)

Whimsical campaigns.

Do you know "Captain Cap"?

No, probably not. Do you suppose, perhaps, that he is a rival or disciple of the famous marksman Ira Paine?

Do so no longer.

Captain Cap is a candidate for parliament in the 2nd district of the 9th arrondissement. To convince yourself of this, you need only glance at the colorful posters that cover the buildings in the neighborhood of Saint-Georges. Captain Cap's are bright red or blue, like lapis lazuli. They carry, in enormous letters, the following words:

ALBERT CAPERON
known as
CAPTAIN CAP
Antibureaucratic and anti-European candidate.

We have tried in vain to meet Captain Cap. Impossible to find him. Nobody knows where this wonderful candidate lives. Does he come from regions dear to the heart of Buffalo Bill? Is he a cowboy, a formidable opponent of the Redskins?

No; we think Captain Cap is an amiable joker. (*Le Gaulois*, August 6, 1893.)

MY CANDIDATE

One cannot deny at this moment that many millions of Frenchmen are perplexed, I above all. I have been annoyed, these past few days, by the thousands of multicolored posters inviting me to read carefully and to choose wisely. Difficult words—imperative mandate, bourgeois hydra, socialist tyranny—danced before my eyes, and I would still be undecided if I had not had the good fortune to encounter a poster for my candidate:

CAPTAIN CAP
the antibureaucratic and anti-European
candidate

Yes, he's the one! I have no reason to conceal my choice, and am not afraid to give his name to the public.

I must admit that at first I was somewhat suspicious: an antibureaucratic and anti-European campaign could cloak disastrous ambitions, and lead to unfortunate consequences. It is always disagreeable to have to become a Patagonian citizen to justify your vote; but, after the public meeting given by Captain Cap, I no longer hesitate to acclaim him fervently; and if I was not the first to unhitch his carriage, it is only because I am afraid of horses, even coach horses.

My candidate, Captain Cap, in his campaign rally, gave his biography himself.

He has an English accent, and was born in Paris, but I suspect his family is from Marseilles.

His past holds great promise for his future: he hunted seals for ten years, stopped ten trains in their tracks—and God knows they go fast in the Far West—and, finally, bettering Jules Verne's fifteen-year-old captain, was already one at twelve!

Such accomplishments are more than enough to assure his election; however, having spoken of what he has done, I must not neglect a few pertinent words on what he will do.

Questioned about his slogan, antibureaucratic and anti-European, Captain Cap affirmed that it meant nothing, and was simply put under his name to look good. This alone proves to me his love of order and regularity.

As for his platform, he has none. A faithful interpreter of the voters, Captain Cap, if elected, will ask his country what it asks of him.

Here, in addition, are the great questions that he has promised to raise in the Chamber:

1. Leveling Montmartre. It this proves too expensive, he will demand that the rest of Paris be raised (always that love of regularity).
2. Establishing a state monopoly on hot water fountains.
3. Decontrolling the price of greasepaint.
4. Digging the great polyglot tunnel.

This last improvement calls for an explanation.

Captain Cap has long been aware of how difficult it is for children to learn languages. With his system, a long tunnel divided into compartments, it will become as easy as catching a cold.

Schools for different languages will be found in each compartment. Every citizen will bring his six-year-old son to the entrance of the vault, and, after ten years, look for him at the other end.

The child, unless deaf and mute, will be fluent in all languages. Ideas such as these spring only from a mind of genius; I am keen on my candidate.

I will go to the polls with confidence, and solemnly deposit his name, convinced of his certain success.

Ah! I forgot one final qualification:

In America, Captain Cap founded an order of which he is the grand master.

His election will probably bring great pleasure to employees of the Post Office; for, according to his declarations, he will work to establish... a Postal Order. (Charles Quinel, *Le Charivari,* August 13, 1893.)

Let us close these excerpts with the short article mentioned earlier, which the late Francisque Sarcey did not hesitate to devote to our friend:

I spent a delightful evening Saturday, in a small social-artistic society called the Gardenia, I'm not sure why, perhaps because the members of the society prefer gardenias to other flowers. They are all charming young people, friendly, well educated, and, above all, passionate about the theater.

Isn't this better, between you and me, than going to some cafe to debase yourself, drink a quantity of refreshments that make you sick to your stomach, and, finally, spend too much money?

The performance took place at the Bodinier theater. Everything went like clockwork.

The play, intelligently composed of short acts and interludes, seemed to charm the brilliant society that comprised the Gardenia's audience. Many pretty women, parenthetically, belonging, I am told, to the Canadian community in Paris.

This comes as no surprise, given that the president of the society is none other than the genial Paul Fabre, son of the high commissioner for Canada in Paris.

To report in detail what was acted, said, or sung, is beyond me. I lost my program, and, well, when I have no more program to consult, you might as well go whistle in the wind.

Suffice it to say that the evening showed much good will and talent, more talent than one sometimes finds in the supposedly serious theater.

One debut particularly interested me, for it was apparently a debut, although I found that hard to believe.

Oh, it was not a large role that drew my attention to the actor. It was a very small role, as a servant, bringing a letter, at three different times.

But I have not yet named my actor: the program called him Cap, but his friends at the Gardenia referred to him as "Captain Cap."

Words cannot express my pleasure at the sober and elegant performance of this Cap. There is in this amateur, mark my words, the germ of something, and it is not without some impatience that I await the next production at the Gardenia. (Francisque Sarcey, *Le Chat Noir*, December 10, 1892.)

After such unimpeachable testimonies, if even one of the ladies and gentlemen of my readership still insists on denying the existence of Captain Cap, I am prepared, when and where you choose, to make it a personal affair. A. A.

Notes:

1. Where our good friend Escudier is currently aedile.

2. How long ago it was! And how many establishments have disappeared since then, or been transformed, or been absorbed by powerful neighbors, such as the picturesque Irish Bar on Royale Street, annexed by the flourishing Brasserie Véber!

3. A few pages further, the reader can judge for himself.

4. It was for us, alas, that the future reserved those same disappointments. Thanks to certain machinations which I will have the good taste not to recall, Mr. Berger prevailed over our brilliant candidate.

5. Mr. Alphonse Allais was not, in fact, in Paris on that day. If memory serves, he was in Normandy, but—let us be fair, above all—the infamous bureaucracy had nothing to do with this displacement.

Translator's Notes

Allais's title for this initial dossier was *Le Captain Cap devant le suffrage universel.* Since universal suffrage then extended only to white men, which is not what it now means, I changed the title for clarity. You may write in the original, if you like.

Originally, the Chat Noir planned to run a candidate in each arrondissement: Paul Verlaine, for example, was slated for the 2nd. Only Captain Cap ended up running, in the 9th, home of many artists, and, of course, many English and American bars.

The Auberge du Clou, Captain Cap's campaign headquarters, was known as an artists' hangout: the name, Nail Inn, came from the fact that artists often paid for drinks by hanging up a picture. Erik Satie played the piano there; it was there that he met Debussy.

A gloss on every name would be excessive; here are a few of the more prominent:

Georges Courteline had quite a long career as a humorist, particularly in the theater. He was also renowned for the invention of the "idiot-meter," a tube filled with alcohol that would drench the unwary.

George Auriol was an old friend of Cap, a poet, graphic artist, and typographer. He preferred the English spelling of his first name, to the eternal despair of proofreaders.

Maurice O'Reilly worked at the Canadian office; he was a friend of Paul Fabre, and a Gardenia regular.

Armand Berthez was an actor, and for many years director of the Théâtre des Capucines. He was also an early member of the Gardenia.

Francisque Sarcey was a popular theater critic; he was also conservative, anti-intellectual, and obese, making him an irresistible target for bohemians. Nobody, however, mocked Sarcey with the determination and invention of Allais. He wrote bawdy columns under Sarcey's name for the Chat Noir's paper, and once declared that only two people had the right to use the name Francisque Sarcey: first, Alphonse Allais, and second, Francisque Sarcey. Sarcey died in 1898; including the review of Cap's theatrical debut was quite a touching tribute on Allais's part, especially since he wrote it himself. The description of Cap's performance as "sober and elegant" should probably also be taken with caution.

PART TWO
The Apparent Symbiosis Between the Boa & Giraffe

CHAPTER I

The adventures of Captain Cap in the region of Upper Niger. The apparent symbiosis between the boa and giraffe, when laryngitis afflicts that quadruped whose neck nature has pleased to elongate.

I had not had the pleasure of seeing my valiant friend Captain Cap since the legislative election that desolated France in 1893.

Do you remember? 176 citizens of the 9th arrondissement (the Saint-Georges quarter) affirmed their staunch anti-European convictions by voting for Captain Cap.

"Hello, Cap!" I said, delighted.

"Hello!" replied Cap.

And he seized my hands with uncommon verve. He called me "old fellow," and introduced me to the gentleman at his side, a well-dressed chap of uncertain age, whom he decorated with the title of *commodore*. He led us off for a drink in a Spanish bodega run by Belgians who sell American drinks. (Another of your tricks, internationalism!)

Cap ordered three *John Collinses*,[1] from under the counter.

And our tongues loosened.

I reproached the intrepid Captain for his long absence.

"I have been very busy," he answered coldly, "these past two months. To begin with, the government of Andorra engaged me to organize a fleet of destroyers..."

I raised my finger to instruct the bartender to replenish our refreshments.

"And then," Cap continued, "I went to Africa, where I have many interests."

"Oh, pish."

"Yes, I was chosen by the administrative council to organize the service."

"What service, Captain?"

"The service of the *General Society for Advertisement in the Toilets of Sudan...* Ah! Africa!"

"Darkest Africa, as Stanley put it."

"Stanley never set his filthy foot in Africa."

"So I suspected."

"The little he knows of the place, he read in a supplement to the *Lanterne*." (?)

The commodore took advantage of a brief lull to order a bottle of champagne (a small extra-dry, and I say no more than that).

Cap continued: "In the *Journal* two or three days ago, my dear Alphonse, you told the story of a young shark who wept when he saw a purse made of his mother's skin. I saw something better the other day in Africa."

"Indeed!"

"Perfectly so! And if you think your shark holds the record for pathos, you've put your foot in it right up to the kneecap!"

"Gracious!"

"You know that in Upper Niger, it's currently the rainy season."

"That detail had escaped me."

"The rainy season, in that part of the world, corresponds fairly precisely to unpleasant periods of humidity."

"I might have guessed."

"And who is particularly bothered by periods of humidity?"

"Here we go!"

"Giraffes. You think you know what a giraffe is, you who know everything."

"I beg your pardon!"

"Beg your own pardon! Giraffes are animals whose necks nature, that great joker, has stretched to a ridiculous height. Thus their unusual propensity for illnesses of the throat and vocal cords. If our operas, comic operas, and even operettas cast only giraffes, we could not even count the canceled performances."

"Quite so."

"And yet no! We could indeed; for giraffes, who rarely use a laryngoscope, for whom potassium chlorate is a myth and cocaine a chimera, giraffes, I tell you, when they fall ill, recover quickly and at little or no expense."

Cap, noticing just then that the bottle of extra-dry was empty, was overcome with a rictus of agonized stupor which the bartender did not misread: he brought another.

"This is how the giraffe does it. She reclines, intoning a sort of plaintive melody which has the property of attracting boa constrictors. The reptile arrives on tiptoe, if you will excuse the expression, and gently, carefully, wraps himself around the young patient's neck, from her shoulders all the way up to her chin. Our elegant Parisian ladies wear boas of fur or feathers. Giraffes wear boas of boa, which is much closer to nature. Forty-eight hours of this treatment, and the giraffe is healthier than ever. Ha! What do you say to that?"

The commodore took the floor: "What I say to that, is that we mustn't read the slightest humanity—or, rather, *giraffity*—into the boa's actions. An inquisitive and gossipy reptile, the boa constrictor is quite frustrated by his limited visual horizon. When he wraps himself around the giraffe's neck, it's just to see farther and higher. That's all! And the giraffe would be quite foolish to show any gratitude to the scoundrel. Bartender, three *corpse revivers*[2]—and immaculately prepared, if you please."

Notes:

1. An excellent drink for languid mornings, the *John Collins* is prepared in the following fashion: fill a large glass with crushed ice, two teaspoons of sugar, the juice of one lemon, and a jigger of gin. Top off with seltzer or soda, pour, and sip with straws.

2. This imaginative recipe is rather difficult to prepare, since the ingredients are of such varying densities. You must pour into a glass, with the aid of a little spoon, taking infinite pains not to mix them, the twelve following liqueurs: grenadine, raspberry, anisette, strawberry, white mint, green Chartreuse, cherry brandy, prunelle, kümmel, guignolet, kirsch, and cognac. Drink in one gulp.

CHAPTER II

*In which we learn how Captain Cap
acquits himself of his amorous debts.*

He—and I do not say "he" lightly—who first stated the lapidary axiom "Good accounts make good neighbors" was no callow youth.

The number of disciples it has guided appears, to me, innumerable. Far from objecting to it, I find myself in complete accord.

My friend Captain Cap brings to my thesis the support of a recent example.

Some time last week, as Captain Cap left a meeting of the "General Union of the Whalers of the Corrèze," of which he is vice president, he met a young courtesan, with whom, for the night, he elected to set up housekeeping.

At dawn, he left the young woman, excusing himself— on God knows what pretext—from paying the cutie.

Only three or four days later, Captain Cap visited Montmulot Observatory, where he is charged especially with the nocturnal surveillance of conjunctional relations, and again met the young lady.

And again, he knew her—in, of course, the Biblical sense of the word.

Early the next morning, as Cap prepared to leave his companion, she decided to ask him for a small sum, which, although nominal, established a troublesome precedent!

So, in his frostiest tones, Cap said, "Excuse me, miss: it is true that I slept with you last Monday."

"..."

"Do not interrupt."

"..."

"But did you not also sleep with me?"

"So?"

"So, we are even."

And Cap returned to his little hotel, suffused with the greatest moral serenity.

CHAPTER III

In which is revealed the existence of Meat-Land, otherwise known as the cold cut mine, a rich quarry of game found near Arthurville (in the province of Quebec).

A t this story, an incredulous smile crossed my lips, and sparkles of amusement twinkled in my eyes. Cap, my interlocutor, showed no reaction; he simply summoned the waiter and ordered "two more," which is the American way to say "more of the same," or, more plainly, "another round."

The waiter, then, brought two more *mint juleps.*[1]

I have known Captain Cap for some time now; I often meet him in one of the many American bars near the Opera House and the Madeleine Church. I am used to his bluff and hyperbole, but this story, really, went beyond the permissible pale of the Canadian joke.

(Canadians are charming children, and, one might say, sort of transatlantic Gascons; and Cap has many Canadian qualities.)

Cap coldly informed me that he had just discovered, six miles from Arthurville (in the province of Quebec), a cold cut mine!

Yes, I heard that correctly, and you read it correctly: a *cold cut mine*, or "Meat-Land," as they call it there.

I resolved to get to the bottom of this, so the next morning I paid a call on the Canadian Consulate, at 10 Rome Street.

In the absence of Mr. Fabre, the amiable consul, I was received—quite graciously, I might add—by his son Paul, and by the honorable Maurice X., a young diplomat of great promise.

"Meat-Land!" these gentlemen cried. "Why, nothing could be more serious! What? You don't believe in Meat-Land?"

I had to confess my skepticism.

The two gentlemen were only too happy to inform me, and I learned that Captain Cap had not exaggerated in the slightest.

Near Arthurville, in the middle of the virgin forest (it was virgin then), lay an enormous bowl-shaped ravine, ringed by steep cliffs, and carpeted (like our Alps) with a thousand varieties of aromatic plants: thyme, lavender, tarragon, laurel, etc.

The forest was populated by moose, antelopes, deer, rabbits, hares, etc.

On one exceptionally hot and dry day, a fire broke out in the forest, and soon spread throughout the region.

Terrified, the unlucky creatures fled, seeking shelter from the inferno.

There was the ravine, with its steep but incombustible cliffs. The animals thought they were saved!

They had not reckoned on the extraordinary heat unleashed by the tremendous blaze.

Moose, antelopes, deer, rabbits, hares, etc., dove in by the thousands, hoping for refuge, and finding only death by suffocation.

They were not only killed, but cooked.

Until the temperature dropped back to normal, all of this meat simmered in its own juices (as in the culinary technique we call "braising").

The heavier parts—bones, horns, skin—sank gently to the bottom of the giant pot. The lighter fat floated to the top, forming a sort of protective crust.

Meanwhile, the little aromatic herbs (like those in our Alps) seasoned the pâté, and made it into a succulent foodstuff.

Let me add that a warehouse for Meat-Land will soon be established in Paris, in the large apartment house at the corner of Martyrs Street and Saint-Michel Avenue.

A society is being formed to market this unique substance. We will return to the subject, a subject of great importance, and one which I will occasionally call to the attention of investors.

Notes:

1. The *mint julep* is excellent, when you can find fresh mint: crush four sprigs of the plant with a teaspoon of sugar, add a glass of cognac, fill with crushed ice, add a jigger of yellow Chartreuse, top off with water, and stir well. Soak a sprig of mint in lemon juice, and put it in the center of the glass. Add seasonal fruits, and pour over it, without stirring, a dash of rum. Sprinkle with sugar. Drink with a straw.

CHAPTER IV

In which is demonstrated, by Captain Cap's example, the vanity of hypnotic science and the futility of auto-suggestive influence.

"For my part," said Dr. V., "the most curious case of auto-suggestion that I ever saw was some five or six years ago. Extremely curious, even!"

"Tell us about it, doctor."

V., whose encyclopedic knowledge is complemented by perfect courtesy, told us the following story:

"We were really hitting the bottle that day. We were celebrating the completion of a friend's thesis, and, my word, we celebrated copiously. Everybody was more or less plastered, but the one who beat all records for intoxication was a comrade of ours, an incoercible sluggard and unbridled troublemaker, whom I will designate with the letter Y., just because.

"Poor Y., at the stroke of midnight, was as stewed as a platter of boarding house prunes. His antics, almost all of questionable taste, got us booted from the local brasseries. Fortunately, the neighborhood contained a virtually complete set of saloons, so very little time elapsed when we were not downing a variety of spirits.

"At the Source, he decided to remove his shoes, and, at the risk of catching a serious cold, take a foot bath in a small tank swimming with crayfish.

"He then ordered a bowl of onion soup, and poured it generously into the tank, on the pretext that gravel was not enough food for the little crustaceans.

"At one moment, drunker than ever, he arose to go who knows where. Thinking that he was leaving the room, he bumped into a mirror, saw his reflection, and then, all hell broke loose!

"'There you are, you swine!' he cried, addressing his reflection. 'Well, aren't you a pretty sight! Congratulations! Here you are, drunk again! Don't deny it! You can barely stand! Well, you scum, whoever sold you all that for a bottle didn't rob you! Oh, don't you look nice, with your jacket open, your tie undone, your collar unbuttoned, your hair all tangled! Aren't you ashamed, at your age?'

"And then, a brief pause, during which he glared at himself with true ferocity. He resumed:

"'And while you carouse around Paris, your parents in the country work to send you money. Scoundrel! Parasite! Scum! Listen to me.'

"And then, still talking to his reflection, he assumed a tone of inexpressible authority!

"'Listen. You are going home to bed, right now. Tomorrow, you will rise early; you will get to work; and you will never set foot in a cafe again. If I ever catch you in a saloon, I will grab you by the scruff of the neck, and throw you out into the street. So, off with you, you pig! And I hope I never see you again!'

"Like a somnambulist, he turned toward us, and took his hat and coat. He left.

"We all thought that he was joking. Not at all! We never saw him in a cafe again. In six months, he passed his final exams and finished his thesis. And today he is a professor at the Faculty of Medicine in Nancy.

"The look he gave himself in the mirror put him into a hypnotic trance; and he suggested to himself, by his own reflection, that he stop drinking and get to work!"

We all listened to this story with great interest. Captain Cap, especially, seemed deeply moved.

"Do you think," he asked the doctor, "that the technique would work with me?"

"Why not?" said Dr. V. "You can always try."

Cap stood up, headed for a mirror, gave himself a terrible look, and began berating himself as the scum of the earth.

Every insult from two continents passed before our ears.

At times Cap insulted himself in French, at times in English, and now and then in a language spoken by a people of whom Cap may be the only member.

Once his repertory was exhausted, Cap collected his hat and coat, and walked out without another word.

"Wouldn't it be funny," one of us said, "if Cap set to work tomorrow morning, and became a professor at the Faculty of Medicine in Nancy!"

Unfortunately, that illusion faded that very evening.

Returning home, and passing the Pousset brasserie, I decided to go in, and see if the Pale Princess, by any chance, might await me.[1]

No Pale Princess! (In someone else's arms, no doubt.) On the other hand, who did I see comfortably installed before an Eiffelesque pile of saucers? You have already guessed. My old friend Captain Cap.

He offered me a pint with all the civility in the world, and added philosophically:

"What can you do? Hypnotism doesn't work with all temperaments."

Notes:

1. Poor little Pale Princess! How long ago it was!

CHAPTER V

In which Captain Cap conducts a contradictory and remarkably unconvincing experiment in hypnotism.

Just then, Captain Cap felt the need to assume an air of mystery. And, as a glimmer of curiosity kindled in our eyes:

"Don't blame me," the Captain said, "I can say no more. My ORDER prohibits it."

Captain Cap belongs to a quite extraordinary Order, whose usefulness is second to none.

Offered any proposition to which he has the slightest objection, Captain Cap coldly protests:

"I am very sorry, my dear chap, but my Order prohibits it!"

And he adds with that smile that is his alone:

"Don't blame me."

Nevertheless, Cap was burning to speak.

We pretended to busy ourselves with other matters, and soon the Captain said:

"An amazing subject!"

Solely so that we might hear the rest of the story, none

of us, Machiavellianally, showed the least interest.

"Imagine," Cap persisted.

Bored did we appear to this insistence.

Then Cap opened the sluices.

It concerned a nice little lady in Montmartre, as pretty as a picture, an amazing little lady!

You could hypnotize her like that, one, two! And there you were!

An amazing subject, I tell you!

Once asleep, she was nothing but soft wax between the fingers of your will; if, that is, you will excuse the expression.

If we liked, we could go that very evening.

We went.

With the rough hand of a seasoned mariner, Cap took the tiny hands of the little Montmartrian shepherdess, and with his other made several passes known to him alone.

One, two, three... That's it! She is asleep.

Then Cap pulled from his pocket a raw potato and a guava.

Having peeled both, he offered the subject a slice of raw potato, saying in a loud voice trembling with suggestion:

"Eat this, it is guava."

No sooner had the child chewed a piece of Parmentier's favorite tuber, when she expressed strong disgust.

She even spat it out, grimacing like the devil.

A smile on his lips, Cap changed the experiment.

This time it was guava that he gave the young lady, saying in a voice of no less authority:

"Eat this, it is a raw potato."

No sooner had the child chewed a morsel of the delicious fruit, when she asked for more.

She finished off the guava.

And if you imagine that Cap was unsettled one iota by this unexpected result, you are gravely mistaken.

As we left the house, the Captain said, with lively scientific interest:

"Curious, eh, the depravity of that girl, who adores raw potato, but can't taste guava?"

CHAPTER VI

In which Captain Cap indicates a simple method to assure European equilibrium.

"Tell me, my dear Allais, have you ever had the urge to incubate kippered herring eggs with a stuffed ostrich?"

"Never, my dear Cap, absolutely never, I swear!"

"And yet, that is exactly the current amusement of Mr. Carnot."[1]

"Mr. Carnot?"

"Mr. Carnot himself."

"Mr. Carnot is incubating kippered herring eggs with stuffed ostriches?"

"Precisely, old man!"

"In that case, Captain, permit me to remark that it's a diversion unworthy of a man of Mr. Carnot's age and position!"

"And what do you suppose the rest of Europe thinks of a Republic whose head of state spends his time incubating kippered herring eggs with stuffed ostriches?"

"Ah! All of that, my poor Cap, will not improve matters."

"Nor lead to disarmament, without which no peace or prosperity is possible."

"Quite so!"

"When I say that Mr. Carnot incubates kippered herring eggs with stuffed ostriches, you must not, of course, take my allegation literally. It's merely an image —a symbol, as Moréas would say."

And, as the bartender served us, for we were extremely depressed, a *gin flip*[2], Captain Cap said:

"We were discussing general disarmament, just now. Do you know what prevents disarmament, even more than the question of Alsace-Lorraine?"

"Tell me, and then I will know."

"What prevents disarmament is our preoccupation with European equilibrium, and European equilibrium hinges entirely on the question of the Dardanelles, and on the question of the Balkans."

"I think so too."

"Do you think them insoluble, these two questions?"

"A delicate problem, at any rate."

"Not so much, my dear Allais, not so much!"

"I am convinced, my dear Cap, that it would be child's play for you; but as for the rest of us...!"

"As you say, child's play... And yet I've spent three years, working on the solution to this double problem!"

"Three years?"

"Yes, three years! For the past three years, thanks to

some admirable maps prepared by my staff, I've been calculating the displacement of the Dardanelles."

"The displacement?"

"Yes, the displacement, or, if you prefer, the volume... Meanwhile, I have also calculated the exact volume of the Balkans."

"All of which is no easy job."

"I know! And I have arrived at the calculation that the volume of the Balkans is essentially the same as the displacement of the Dardanelles."

"So that?"

"So that, it's quite simple! I shove the Balkans into the Dardanelles, and there you are!"

"And with it my congratulations, Cap!"

"Thus, the Balkans are leveled, the Dardanelles are filled up, and no more Dardanelles, no more Balkans! No more vexing problems for European equilibrium! Peace is assured, with disarmament, prosperity, happiness for all."

"And do you really think, Cap, that England would permit it?"

"England?"

Here Cap became mysterious. He looked furtively around us, assuring himself that no suspect ear was on the alert.

"England?" he repeated. "I have it on good authority that if England so much as lifts its little finger, yes, its *little-fin-ger*, Peloponnisos is prepared to teach it a lesson."

"Peloponnisos?"

"In alliance with Jutland, that is."

Notes:

1. Poor Mr. Carnot! How long ago it was!

2. In a glass of cracked ice, add two teaspoons of sugar, a fresh egg yolk, a small amount of *crème de noyaux*, and top off with Old Tom Gin. Shake, strain, pour, and sprinkle with nutmeg. An excellent stimulant when the temperature drops, this *gin flip*.

CHAPTER VII

In which Captain Cap gives a masterful lesson in savoir-faire to an ignorant, European, and dimwitted bartender.

Although it was, truth to tell, still early in the day, a raging thirst choked both Captain Cap and me (the unhappy consequence, no doubt, of the previous night's debauch).[1]

With one accord, we quickly dismounted our tandem, and gazed toward the horizon.

Immediately, a large and fashionable cafe presented itself.

Despite its disturbingly European appearance, we decided to drink there.

"Send me a steward!" ordered Cap.

"At your service, sir," bowed the manager.

"Give us two big glasses."

"Here, sir."

"I said *two big glasses*, not *two thimbles*. Give us two big glasses."

"Here, sir."

"Finally. And now, some sugar."

"Here, sir."

"No, not these ludicrous little lumps of sugar. Granulated sugar."

"Here, sir."

"And not this Havana sugar that stinks of tobacco."

"But, sir..."

"I demand granulated sugar from Barbados. It alone is fit for the drink I plan to prepare."

"This is all we have."

"Sad! Very sad! Well..."

And Cap tossed into our glasses a few spoonfuls of sugar, which he moistened with a drop of water.

"And now, two lemons!"

"Here, sir."

Cap eyed the lemons with profound contempt.

"Do you call these lemons?"

"But, sir..."

"Bring me two other lemons."

"Here, sir."

At this, Cap flew into a genuine rage.

"I said two *other* lemons! Do you understand? Two *other* lemons! Two *other*! Not *two more*, but *two other*! Two lemons other than those which you had the effrontery to set before me. You dump these goddam Sicilian lemons on me! And I yearn only for lemons from the Island of Rhodes. Do you have any lemons from the Island of Rhodes?"

"Not at the moment."

"Oh, that's just wonderful. Well..."

And Cap squeezed some juice from the Sicilian lemons into our glasses.

"Some gin now! What gin do you have?"

"Anchor Gin and Old Tom Gin."

"Genuine Anchor?"

"Genuine."

"Genuine Old Tom?"

"Genuine."

"And Young Charley Gin? Do you have that?"

"I don't know it."

"You don't know anything. Well..."

And Cap poured us both a generous (oh, how generous!) bumper of Old Tom Gin.

"Now to mix it!" he added.

With the help of a long spoon, we stirred the beginning of the mixture.

"And now, some ice!"

"Here, sir."

"This is ice?"

"But of course, sir!"

"Where did you get this ice?"

"From the Auteuil factory, sir!"

"The Auteuil factory? It may be admirably outfitted to supply hot water to the people of Paris, but it doesn't know the first thing about refrigeration. You can tell it from me..."

"But, sir!"

"Besides, I know of only one ice worthy of the name: that which is collected in winter from the Barbotte."

"Oh!"

"Yes, from the Barbotte! The Barbotte is a little river that flows into the Richelieu, which Richelieu flows into the Saint Lawrence. And do you know the name of the little town found at the confluence of the Richelieu and Saint Lawrence?"

"My word, sir..."

"Ah, you're not up on your geography, you Europeans! The little town found at the confluence of the Richelieu and Saint Lawrence is called Sorel. And, whatever you do, don't confuse Sorel in Canada with the lovely and alluring Cécile Sorel, nor with Albert Sorel, the distinguished and amiable academician! Nor with his son, Albert-Emile Sorel! Swear to me that you will not confuse them!"

"Gladly, sir."

"Well then, give me your filthy ice from the Auteuil factory."

"Here, sir."

And Cap dropped a few of the imitation icebergs into our beverages.

"And the last thing I need from you is two bottles of soda. What soda do you stock here?"

"Why, the best! *Schweppes!*"

"Father, if thou be willing, remove this cup from me! *Schweppes*! Of course, it's not a contemptible brand, but compared to the soda made by my old friend Moonman in Fall-River, Schweppes is a muddy, brackish, and noxious beverage! Well... bring us Schweppes!"

"And mind the steps," I poetized.

It was done! All that was left was to quaff our drinks, in great drafts, like men who are free, strong, dynamic, and as dry as a bone... when the manager had the forever regrettable idea to bring us straws, and perfectly fine ones at that.

Cap's temper asked for nothing more.

"You call these straws!" he exploded.

"But, sir..."

"No! These aren't straws! They're just straw, and wilted straw at that, pulled out from under some no doubt unspeakable cows! I am not accustomed to having my drink contaminated with manure. Let us leave, my friend, let us leave!"

And Cap tossed a hundred sous onto the counter; and we left for the next bar, where we enjoyed ourselves immensely with a carafe of white wine, a little gum syrup, and a half bottle of seltzer!

Notes:

1. It is true: I sometimes drank more than my thirst required. How long ago it was! And how ashamed I am of my past! If only I can serve as an example to the youth of today!

CHAPTER VIII

In which Cap successfully investigates the true name of an orangutan wrongly designated as Auguste.

On arriving in Nice, Captain Cap and I, two posters disputed the glory of attracting our attention.

(The sentence that I have just written is of rather dubious syntax. One would think that I had not done my humanities.)

Of the poster that charmed me, myself, here is the gist:

X., CHIROPODIST
SOME ADDRESS, SOME STREET
THE ONLY SERIOUS CHIROPODIST IN NICE

Never, as at that moment, have I so mourned the absence of corns, callouses, blisters, or other stratagems on my extremities.

To have at hand an artist who, not content to be serious, claims to be the *only* serious in such an important community as Nice, and to have no reason to employ him! Regrettable, oh how!

Cap proposed a technique that is traditional among the women in some Polynesian archipelago, who find beauty in having as many corns as possible, on those parts of the body least suitable for the purpose.

I declined the offer, judging the game not worth the candle, and we turned to another form of amusement.

The flyer that Cap preferred announced that at Urbi, Orbi, and Co. any individual, possessing a small sum varying between 25 centimes and one franc, could enjoy the spectacle of an orangutan, also known, ladies and gentleman, as the veritable man of the woods, the ONLY (like my chiropodist at the beginning) to have appeared in France since quite some time ago.

An engraving accompanied the text, an engraving depicting the bust of the quadrumane; and around the engraving, like an inscription on a medallion, ran these words, circularly:

My name is Auguste:
10,000 francs to whoever can prove the contrary!

Ten thousand francs to whoever can prove the contrary!

The contrary of what? That the beast in question is a true orangutan, an authentic man of the woods, or simply that his real name is Auguste?

To the limpid soul of Cap, there could be no doubt.

All we had to do was demonstrate that the ridiculous

monkey was not named Auguste, collect the 500 louis, and go break the bank at Monte Carlo!

My God, it was none too complicated!

And Cap never stopped repeating:

"I don't know, something tells me that orangutan's name is not Auguste."

"Indeed!"

"Why indeed? That filthy gorilla doesn't look like he's named Auguste."

"Indeed!"

"Allais, if you say 'indeed' one more time, I will slam a boat paddle across your piehole!"

Anything across the piehole but a boat paddle! This is my motto.

I dropped the matter, and we spoke of other things, nursing a *Manhattan cocktail* in perfect amity.[1]

That very evening, Cap left for Antibes on his yacht, *King of the Madrepores*, and I didn't see him again for a fortnight.

One morning, I was awakened by loud shouts in my antechamber; the walls shook with the Captain's clarion cries of triumph.

"Aha!" proclaimed Cap. "I have it, I have the proof!"

"What proof?" I asked, stretching on my bed.

"I knew damn well that nasty chimpanzee wasn't named Auguste!"

"Ah!"

"I just received a despatch from Borneo, his native city. Not only is his name not Auguste, it's Henry!"

"Heavens, that's serious. And tell me, my dear Cap, do you think that Henry the ape, of Nice, is related to Henry the Eighth, of England?"

"In your conduct, my dear Alphonse, the ridiculous vies with the odious... I have received from our consul in Borneo all of the documents establishing, incontestably, that the ape in Pont-Vieux is named Henry. So, out of bed, and off to an attorney. Ten thousand francs await us!"

My notary in Nice, Mr. Pineau, regarded as one of the finest jurisconsults in the Alpes-Maritimes, gave us the address of an excellent attorney, and our stamped paper was ready in less time than it takes to write it.

But alas! The little country fair in Pont-Vieux had closed.

The spurious Auguste, his booth, his barker, had all moved to San Remo, on Italian soil; and Italian law is very strict on the matter: it is strictly forbidden to investigate the civil status of any monkey 70 centimeters or taller.

Notes:

1. An exquisite aperitif, this *Manhattan cocktail*: mix equal parts of whiskey and Turin vermouth, add a few drops of angostura and a small spoonful of Curaçao. Crushed ice. Shake, strain, and pour.

CHAPTER IX

Résumé—too brief, alas!—of a talk by Captain Cap proposing a new division of France.

You have certainly noticed, ladies and gentlemen, that we give the name "Midi"—that is, "Noon"—to the meridional section of France. I go to the Noon. I come from the Noon. His doctors advised him to spend winter in the Noon. He has a Noon accent, etc., etc. These are common expressions that we hear every day, and which none of us, I wager, ever thinks of protesting, so natural have they become.

But why, I ask you?

Why does the south alone benefit from this designation, while no other part of France is called *Midnight* or *A quarter to four*?

I repeat, this state of affairs does not answer to the ideals of justice that we cherish in our hearts; and I have the honor of introducing a little plan that will eliminate such flagrant partiality.

I divide France (figuratively, that is, since it's already divided enough as it is, the poor dear) into twelve latitudinal slices, each named after an hour of the clock.

The *Noon* will still be the *Noon*; the slice above it will be called *Eleven o'clock*, the one above that *Ten o'clock*, and so on, moving north.

The last slice (*ultima ratio*), farthest to the north, will consequently be called *One o'clock*.

Each of these slices will be further divided into 60 little mini-slices, each representing a minute.

This terminology may strike you as somewhat bizarre, since you're unfamiliar with it; but the first time someone said, "I'm from the Noon," it also seemed funny, you can be sure.

But there's more: just as we cut France across, we will now divide it up vertically, that is to say, along the longitudes.

We thus form seven zones, each named after a day of the week, beginning with the area around Brest, which we will call *Monday*, and ending with the eastern border, which will answer to the name of *Sunday*.[1]

We establish in this way ever so many little squares, whose names alone indicate their positions precisely, much more clearly than with that foolish and outmoded system of longitudes and latitudes.

Paris, for example, if I am not mistaken, will be found at *Thursday—Twenty after five*.

My plan, as you can see, is a simple one; too simple, in fact, to be adopted by the gentlemen of the government.

I can imagine the face of the director of the Bureau of Longitudes.

Have you ever, in Barcelona, seen a big cheese shrug his shoulders? (*General hilarity.*)

Notes:

1. Ah yes, what a beautiful Sunday it will be when the eastern border... but *motus!* Let us always think it, but never say it.

CHAPTER X

An account of the methods employed by Captain Cap to win the record for the millimeter and the record for "wallops." Cap, world champion!

"What's this I hear, my dear Cap? You hold the record for the millimeter?"

"Perfectly so, old chap, you have not been misinformed. I do indeed hold the current record for the millimeter, not only in France, but in Europe and America as well. An Australian has just beaten me, apparently, but my excellent friend and colleague Recordman advises me to await confirmation of that supposed upset.

"I offer with pleasure the details that you request.

"The machine that I ride is a wooden velocipede, constructed in '64 by a wheelwright in Pont-l'Evêque, who, sadly, has since passed away. The model has become rather scarce on the market, and I know of nobody now with a machine like mine, except Mr. Paul de Gaultier de la Hupinière, one of the merriest esthetes in Flers (Ornes).

"At the time that these machines were built, Dunlop was a mere boy and Michelin not yet weaned, so the tires were provisionally replaced by a thin band of sheet metal, which, although perhaps less supple than rubber, can claim the advantage of greater durability.

"To sheet metal, my dear friend, stones in the road are child's play, and broken bottles not even a diversion.

"I hold the *record for the millimeter* on both track and road.

"I won it on the track, without trainers, in less than 1/17,000 of a second.

"On the road, my time was slightly slower: 1/14,000 of a second.

"I should add that, during my last attempt, I had a strong wind against me, as well as a torrential rain. And then—although perhaps I should pass over this detail in silence—my trainers, Mr. X. and Mr. Y.,[1] following the probably excessive consumption of *whiskey stone fences*,[2] found themselves dead drunk, to their surprise.

"Besides, I expect to beat my own record, next September.

"To prepare, I am training seriously, working fourteen hours a day, half on a scatter rug (depicting a tiger in the jungle), and half on wet sand.

"My diet consists exclusively of parboiled stockfish, washed down with couch-grass tea, cut with cherry stems.

"How do I sit on the machine, you ask?

"On this matter, I follow an old proverb from the School of Salerno, which my grandmother often repeated when I was a boy, and which I have never ceased to appreciate:

As rigid as a cyclamen
Sit you upon the cycle, men!

"Consequently, I avoid hunching over the handlebars, and my entire body, without a trace of affectation, approaches the vertical.

"And there, my dear Allais, are the details that you have solicited from my celebrated amiability, and from my courtesy whose praise it were superfluous to sing.

"For additional information, please consult my upcoming work (at press now) *Cupid and Cycle*."

"I wouldn't miss it."

"But this record is not the only one that I can claim. My hard work has also earned me, barring earlier claims, the record for *wallops*."

"*Wallops?*"

"Precisely!"

And Cap explained himself as follows:

"For a cyclist, knowing how to stay on the machine is of great importance; but knowing how to fall perhaps even more so. Anyone of intelligence can see that.

"Thanks to conscientious daily practice, I have obtained the following results on the track:

"18 3/8 falls a minute, 1,097 falls an hour; 69 per meter, and 7,830 per kilometer.

"My method: I started by wrapping myself in cushions made from old tires, which I then gradually deflated. Then, I slowly re-inflated them, replacing the air with bicycle bearings.

"Today, I am in peak condition, and fell yesterday onto a pile of bottles, which I shattered without suffering a single scratch. My machine: a simple handcart wheel, with a counterweighted handlebar, to facilitate falls. Fixed axis. Never any oil."

Other details followed, which might prove tedious to the reader unfamiliar with technical speculations.

Captain Cap will make himself available to any challenger who cares to propose a *wallop* match.

The record for descending six flights of stairs is also held, if we are to believe him, by our intrepid and athletic friend.

"By inclination as well as hygiene, I am an inveterate pedestrian. The Wandering Jew, whom you worship so, is a lazy stick-in-the-mud compared to me.

"There can be no serious sport, of course, without trainers. Now, my current meager resources prevent hiring one.[3]

"So, what did I do? I decided to take as a trainer the first person I see, the last person I see, anyone at all, you, General Brugère, Rev. Lemire, Carolus Duran, it makes no difference.

"I follow the chosen individual, and off I go.

"The chosen individual soon notices my stratagem. He accelerates his pace. I mine. And then we're off, at a good clip.

"Occasionally, I happen on an individual ill-suited for this type of solidarity. Canes splinter across my countenance, heavy hands weigh on my features. More often than not, I return home, bearing a face that is no more than a bleeding, lacerated pulp.

"All excellent things for preserving my record for *wallops*!

"And what of it?

"But I have strayed from my record. I must return to it. First, though, would you care for a little *thunder*?"[4]

"With pleasure."

"Yesterday, I decided to take, instead of a trainer, a traineress.

"A pretty little blonde, in fact!

"And we were off!

"Unfortunately, I became somewhat carried away in the final sprint, and galloped up six flights behind my little blonde in less time than it takes to write it, only to fall upon the little blonde's husband.

"Or rather, the little blonde's husband fell upon me.

"Without losing my composure, I consulted my watch at that very moment. It was 5:17 and 34 seconds.

"When I reached the bottom of the stairs, curiosity impelled me to check the time again. It was exactly 5:17 and 41 seconds.

"Simple subtraction informed me that I had devoured the little blonde's six flights in seven seconds, making a little more than one second per floor."

"Which is, between us, my dear Cap, a splendid performance."

"And one which I will strive to better."

Notes:

1. In the original text, the names of these gentlemen were given in full. But since that time, one of them has received a ten year sentence, and the other has entered a monastery. How long ago it was!

2. The *whiskey stone fence* is simply an excellent cider, sweetened and beaten, into which you pour a glass of Irish or Scotch whiskey. You can also replace those spirits with calvados.

3. It was, in fact, around this time that imprudent speculations in shrew pelts led Cap to the brink of bankruptcy.

4. A great stimulant, the *thunder*: cracked ice, a half teaspoon of sugar, a whole fresh egg, and a jigger of old cognac. Add a generous pinch of cayenne pepper. Beat, strain, and drink.

CHAPTER XI

*Captain Cap's new plan for
interstellar communication.*

The unusual brightness of Mars—due solely, incidentally, to the adoption of the Auer lamp[1] by the planet's inhabitants—has put back on the table the always interesting question of interstellar communication.

If other planetary populations really do crawl in the bosoms of the neighboring stars, how can we signal to them, and inform them that earth, our dear little earth, is peopled with intelligent beings (I speak here of my readers) perfectly capable of communication?

Charles Cros was preoccupied with this question, and published a curious little treatise, in which he proposed a system of light signals, beginning with a simple rhythm, and progressing to more complicated patterns, which could be seen and understood by any creature with a cerebral organization similar to ours.

All of which is very lovely, but if you want to signal to others, you must first alert them to the fact, or, at least, be sure that you have their attention when you try to reach them.

If you see a friend, for example, on the other side of the street, and hope to exchange a few piquant observations, how do you attract his attention?

With a bold gesture? That would be ideal if he was looking at you, but what if he wasn't?

By calling to him?

That's what I wanted you to say!... By calling to him.

If the Martians or Selenites have their backs to us, we must cry out very loudly indeed to make them turn around.

You can see my plan.

To mobilize, for one hour, the entire human race, all animals, bells, pistols, rifles, cannons, deliberating bodies, orchestras, from the Lamoureux to the municipal marching band of Honfleur and the bugle corps of the Queen of Madagascar, etc., etc., pianos, mothers-in-law, in short, every being or object that can make a sound.

At the same hour (or rather, the same *instant*, because the hour is relative), the entire world, animals and people alike, would start to howl like banshees, all the bells in the world would ring, pistols, guns, and cannons would shoot, etc., etc.

This pretty little hullabaloo would last for an hour.

After which, everyone would return home for a well deserved break, and rest his or her ears, if by chance they were still attached.

Then we would wait.

Mars being ... miles from earth, and sound traveling ... miles a second, the Martians would hear our concert after ... hours, ... minutes, and ... seconds.

After twice that amount of time had elapsed, plus the time needed to organize a reply, if we then heard no astral clamor, it would mean either that the Martians are deaf, like proverbial posts, or that they don't care about us, and would rather stick to their own business (Martinis).

And that would be enough to put you off astronomy.

Notes:

1. A more successful invention than its predecessor, developed with his colleague Chopin; the Chopin-Auer lamp gave only a dim and lugubrious light.

CHAPTER XII

An incredible but true account of animal training, accomplished with ease by patient bipeds.

Last Sunday, at the Auteuil racetrack, I ran into Captain Cap; and was particularly delighted, given that I believed our congenial navigator headed for Bilbao.

Last Sunday has not yet so crumbled into the abyss of History that we cannot recall the abominable weather that raged that day.[1]

"In a gale like this," concluded the Captain after the usual greetings, "I would rather drop anchor in the comfort of the Australian Wine Store on Eylau Avenue. Do you share my opinion?"

"I am in complete accord, Captain."

"Well then, let's scram!"

And we scrammed.

"What am I to serve you gentlemen?" asked the pleasant little barmaid.

"Ah! In fact," said Cap, "what shall we have to drink?"

"As for me," I said, "it rains in my heart as it rains on

the town, so I will treat myself to a nice little *angler's cocktail.*"[2]

"There's an idea! I too will treat myself to a nice little *angler's cocktail*. Prepare for us, madam, two nice little *angler's cocktails*, if you please."

Just then, into the bar came a man whom Cap knew, and whom he introduced.

I didn't quite catch his name, but his occupation, should I live as long as a passel of patriarchs, I shall never forget.

Cap's friend bore the modest title of bandmaster of the GOUBET![3]

This strange official told a story that was stranger still.

He had spent the summer, he claimed, training mussels.

"The mussel in no way deserves its traditional reputation for stupidity. However, you do need to proceed gently, since they're exceptionally timid mollusks. With kindness and music, you can work wonders."

"You don't say!"

"Word of honor! I who address you now (and Captain Cap can tell you if I'm the joking type), I have succeeded, by playing Spanish airs on the guitar, in coaxing mussels to accompany me on castanets."

"Now that's what I call an achievement!"

"Let me clarify!... I cannot claim that the mussels actually played castanets: but with a repeated click of the valve, they could imitate them, and in perfect time, I assure you. There is no more comical sight, gentlemen, than a rock covered with such rhythmic mussels!"

"I imagine that it would be no banal spectacle."

During the whole of the bandmaster's story, Cap had nothing to offer, but his troubled expression did not bode well.

He roared:

"Why, that's nothing, training mussels! Mere child's play! I once saw something ten times better!"

The bandmaster of the *Goubet* could not suppress a start.

"Ten times better? Ten times?"

"A thousand times! In California, I saw a fellow who trained birds to sit on telegraph wires, according to the notes he assigned them."

"That would seem to require further explanation."

"Here it is. My man chose a telegraph line with five wires, which represented the staff of a musical score. Each bird was trained to represent a *do*, a *re*, a *mi*, etc. For the rhythm, white birds represented *half notes*, black birds *quarter notes*, smaller birds *eighth notes*, and even smaller birds *sixteenth notes*. My man took it no further than that."

"It's already not bad!"

"He proceeded in this way: accompanied by enormous baskets housing his feathered subjects, he arrived at the place chosen for his demonstration. After opening a special little basket, he indicated the key in which the piece would be performed. A snake crawled from the special little basket, wound itself around the telegraph pole, and slithered up to the wires, which it coiled around to mimic either a *bass* or *treble* clef. The trainer then began to play the piece on a wickerwork trombone."

"Excuse me for interrupting, Cap. What kind of trombone?"

"Wickerwork. Are you unaware that the peasants of California are adept at the art of weaving slide trombones from rods of willow?"

"I only passed through California, with no leisure for ethnographic details."

"So, at each note emitted by the instrument, a bird flew up and sat in the proper place. When the entire little community was in position, the concert began, each bird contributing its note in turn."

The little barmaid[4] at the Australian Wine Store appeared overjoyed at Cap's fantastic imagination, and, as we seemed somewhat dubious, came to his defense with these solemn words:

"Everything the Captain said is absolutely true. I myself have seen those musical birds. They were on the telegraph line between *Urjoquingville* and *Scruebahl Town*, weren't they, Captain?"

Notes:

1. What was true then is false today, and few people now remember the deplorable climatic conditions on that day. After the rain, blue skies.

2. Are you like me? I adore the *angler's cocktail*. Taste it, and you will see: crushed ice, a few drops of angostura, a teaspoon of orange bitters, another of raspberry syrup; top off with gin, shake, strain, and enjoy.

3. At this time, the *Goubet* was considered the vanguard of French submarine design.

4. Oh, how madly in love I was with that woman! Brunette, a bit plump, and so fresh! As downy as a dozen peaches, I can see her now! How long ago it was!

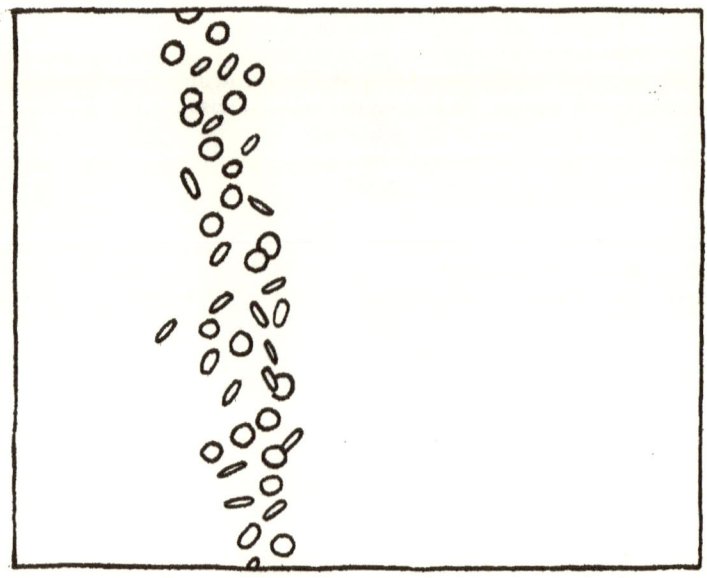

CHAPTER XIII

An idle, and consequently detailed, description of the meticulous and effective procedure by which old confetti is made new.

In a single swallow, Cap downed the large tumbler of *American grog*[1] he had been served, and said to me:

"So, you're not bothered by the painful uncertainty in which you flounder?"

"What painful uncertainty, Captain?"

"To know where waning moons go?"

"Me! Let me assure you, Cap, that waning moons are perfectly free to go where they please, and that I won't be the one to question them!"

As if his ear were granite, Cap persisted:

"And the snows of yesteryear too, my poor friend! No anguish racks you about their destiny?"

"As a fish about an apple, so do I care about the snows of yesteryear... Ah! Certainly, Cap, I am haunted by a memory, but of a more human kind, and I suffer from it!"

I thought that Cap would take an interest in my suffering, and would inquire. Ah! Not a chance!

"And what about old confetti?" he continued, implacable. "Don't you care about them?"

This time, I changed my line of defense, and, to thwart his insistence, feigned a prodigious interest in old confetti.

"Ah! Old confetti!" I cried, my eyes wide. "What happens to old confetti?"

Cap stood his ground.

"I will tell you what happens to old confetti."

And, to encourage him, I asked the bartender to serve us, for I had just caught a bad cold, two immaculately prepared *ale flips*.[2]

"Old confetti! There are no old confetti, or, rather, there will be no longer."

"Do tell! And why this phenomenon?"

"Because of the *New Central Society for the Reclamation of Parisian Confetti*, where I preside over the Administrative Council."

"Tell me more!"

"There is nothing more curious than the operation of this industry. I have just left the factory, and am amazed."

"Details, Captain, please!"

"Here they are, in a few words. The day after Mardi Gras or other festive occasions, our employees, equipped with special tools, collect all of the confetti strewn about the sidewalks of Paris, and take them to our office, at 237 Mazagran Street."

"Good."

"The confetti undergo a preliminary operation called *sorting*, in which the dry are separated from the wet. The former continue to the ventilator, which rids them of dust: this is called *dusting*."

"I might have guessed!"

"All they need then is *pressing*, a process which consists of..."

"Pressing."

"Precisely! With a little iron heated to a certain temperature. The wet confetti remain. They are then transferred, with large epicycloidal hoppers, into vast ovens, where they are dried."

"And this is called *drying*, I suppose?"

"Precisely! Once dried, the confetti are projected violently into a box, shaped vaguely like a parallelepiped. The box is furnished with a barely perceptible slot, through which the little paper discs fly out, one by one. As they exit, each is seized by a miniature articulated pincer, and subjected to the action of a pretty little vibrating brush. This is called..."

"*Brushing*."

"Precisely! Another selection is required. Some of the brushed confetti are soiled with grease, due to their contact with household waste. These last are carefully separated from the others."

"And this is called *separating*."

"Precisely! The soiled confetti are soaked in a solution of potassium carbonate, which saponifies the fatty material and renders it soluble. The last step is to rinse them with fresh water, to wash off all alkaloids. We accomplish this by..."

"*Rinsing with fresh water.*"

"Precisely! So, they are then put back in the oven, ironed, and..."

"And there you are!"

"Do you think that's the end of it?"

"Oh dear!"

"Well, you're wrong. The operation has barely begun."

A glimmer of fear showed in my eyes.

"Are you unaware," continued Cap, "how painful it can be to receive confetti in your mouth or eyes?"

"Believe me, I've had it happen."

"From now on, this martyrdom will be entirely salutary. The confetti, soaked in various liquids, will acquire different densities. The heavier ones will fall into the mouth, the lighter ones into the eyes (which, parenthetically, took some difficult calculation)."

"I can believe it."

"The confetti meant for the mouth are infused with essences conducive to the proper functioning of the respiratory tract."

"And let me guess: those meant for the eyes are impregnated with substances to improve our visual organs."

"Ah! One can hide nothing from you!"

"To your health, my dear Cap."

"God keep you, my dear Allais."

Notes:

1. Heat one part aged rum and one part water, add sugar, and serve with a slice of lemon stuck with four cloves. Warming and stimulating.

2. If you are catching a cold, there is nothing like an *ale flip*. This is how to make it. Heat a half glass of pale ale; separately, mix an egg with a tablespoon of sugar, and sprinkle with nutmeg. After beating the mixture well, pour slowly into the beer, stirring vigorously. This drink is like an eggnog with beer.

CHAPTER XIV

Captain Cap and national defense. A new way to deliver messages. General Dragomirov's objection.

The first human being I saw, as I left the station, was my old friend Captain Cap, walking along Amsterdam Street, lost in thought.

In anticipation of this meeting, the hand of God had already placed in readiness the Irish Bar, run by our old friend Austin.[1]

And it had been so hot since that lunchroom in Serquigny, on my last stop!

We entered.

Eight months had elapsed since I had seen the Captain! Eight months!

A fortunate meeting! And what a pleasant aroma of Old Tom Gin perfumed the cool little bar!

"Give me your hand, Captain, that I may shake it again."

"And give me yours, you lazy rascal."

"No accusations, Cap."

"Yes, I know..."

The Captain had so much to tell me that he didn't know

where to begin.

I came to his assistance.

"You're in your traveling clothes, Captain. Where are you coming from?"

"I was attending military maneuvers in the East."

"Were they a fine spectacle?"

"Oh, I had no time to see the troops! I had other things to do."

"I'm glad you haven't changed, Captain! Nobody else on earth, except the blind, would attend maneuvers without casting an eye on the troops."

"I was only in contact with the commanders-in-chief, Zurlinden, Félix Faure, and Dragomirov."[2]

"You're certainly well connected, Cap!"

"Let us say, rather, that the gentlemen were pleased to meet me."

"Did they appreciate you, at least?"

"They did indeed, my invention being one that commands admiration even from the top brass."

"Your invention, Cap?"

"Yes, my invention."

"Aha!"

That "aha" hid my intolerable itch to know about my friend's invention.

But he retreated into an inexorable cloister of silence.

"Come now, Cap, be kind! A few words about your invention."

"Impossible!"

"At least tell me what it's about."

"Impossible! Impossible! It would compromise our national security."

"Our national security! The well-being of the Fatherland! And to think that you're the one spouting this nonsense. You, Cap, the apostle of anti-Europeanism!"

"France's well-being interests me no more than a game of poker dice,[3] but I'm quite fond of poker dice."

I arose, held out my hand to Cap, and said with emotion:

"*Au revoir*, Cap. Or rather, *adieu*."

"*Adieu*? Why *adieu*?"

"Because I cannot see a friend whose trust I've lost."

"All right, sit down, you big baby. I'll tell all! But you must swear that not a word will leave this room."

"I swear!"

"My idea, like all ideas of genius, is breathtakingly simple. I propose to replace, for the delivery of military communications, pigeons with fish."

"Flying fish?"

"No, just fish that swim around, like other fish. The fish is far more trainable than the pigeon (which, as its name indicates, is an imbecile). Furthermore, it's the soul of discretion. Have you ever heard a fish gossip about its neighbors?"

"Never, Cap!"

"The fish is ideal for the role of military messenger. It carries letters from one general to another, more faithfully, dependably, and quickly than any foolish pigeon."

"And yet nobody thought of it before!"

"People are so stupid."

"Were your maneuvers in the East successful?"

"Absolutely! My team of traveling fish performed a great service for Saussier. Félix Faure was astonished."

"And Dragomirov? What did he say?"

"Dragomirov was furious! He claims that when fish carry messages, it spoils the caviar."

Notes:

1. Our old friend Austin no longer runs the bar, but the people who replaced him seem nice. They're Swiss, I believe.

2. That doesn't make us younger!

3. A dice game similar to poker with cards.

CHAPTER XV

The question of polar bears before Captain Cap.

I would need the pencil of Callot, seconded by the pen of Pierre Maël, to give even a faint idea of the emotion that gripped both of us, Captain Cap and myself, when we saw one another after three long months of separation.

Our hands met in a fervent clasp, and remained long intertwined. We could barely contain our tears.

Cap broke the silence; and his first words were to console me on my return to this bureaucratous and mephitic Europe, and especially this burlesque France, where, in the Captain's forceful words, *you are forbidden to be yourself.*

Cap spoke as much to hide his real emotions, as to express, in decisive terms, his legitimate grievances.

And so it was that we arrived, eventually, at the Australian Wine Store, on Eylau Avenue, where there is a little barmaid who looks like a sweet, plump, Chilean baby.

Our emotions must have left their mark on our features; for the bartender prepared for us, before we even asked, two *brandy cocktails*[1], a drink mandated by the circumstances.

A gentleman was already seated at the bar, before a copious bumper of *Irish whiskey*, softened with a touch of water. *Irish whiskey* with too much water is almost tasteless.

Cap knew the gentleman, and introduced us.

"The honorable Baron Labitte de Montripier."

I adore Cap's various acquaintances. I almost always find in them a picturesque quality that I rarely encounter elsewhere.

The baron had, apparently, just filed a patent with which he expected to amass a princely sum.

Thanks to previously secret techniques, the baron had succeeded in removing from rubber that elasticity that makes it unfit for so many purposes. If necessary, he could make it as fragile as glass. Where will modern industry end, my God? Where will it end?

When we had exhausted the topic of frangible rubber, the conversation turned to health.

The baron contemplated our *brandy cocktails*, and made an observation that plunged Cap into a dark and sudden rage:

"You know, Captain, it's very bad for the stomach to drink so much ice."

"Ice, bad for the stomach? You are either dead drunk, baron, or devoid of all moral sense, to utter such an absurdity, as blasphemous as it is irrational!"

"But..."

"But nothing! Do you know any animal as vigorous and healthy as the polar bear of the arctic region?"

"???"

"You don't, do you? Well, do you think polar bears drink hot tea three times a day? Hot tea on the ice floes? You're completely mad, my dear baron!"

"Excuse me, Captain, I never said..."

"And it's a good thing you didn't, for you'd be the laughing stock of all rational humanity. The polar bears of the arctic region drink nothing but ice water, and it suits them admirably, for their rude health is legendary. Don't we say: *As strong as a polar bear?*"

"Of course."

"And, while we're on the subject of polar bears, will you permit me, my dear Allais, and you, my dear Labitte de Montripier, to reveal a fact unknown by naturalists, since I've never told it to anyone?"

"That would be fortunate for us, Captain, as well as an honor."

"Do you know why polar bears are white?"

"Gracious!"

"Polar bears are white because they're old."

"But the young...?"

"There are no young polar bears. All polar bears are old bears, just as all men with white hair are old men.

"I researched it myself. The bear, in general, is an extremely informed plantigrade, and quite knowledgeable about everything concerning its health and well-being. As soon as any bear, brown, black, or gray, feels the effects of age, as soon as he sees the first white hairs in his fur, oh! well then, he heads north at once; for he knows there's only one way to prolong his days, and that's ice water. You heard me, Montripier: ice water!"

"All of this is very curious, Captain!"

"And the proof is that you never see old bears, or bear skeletons, in any country of the world. Have you ever hiked in the Pyrenees?"

"Rather often."

"Well! Hand on your heart: have you ever seen an old bear, or a bear corpse, in your path?"

"Never."

"Ah! You see what I mean. All bears head north, to grow old, and to die with dignity in the polar region."

"So, we could call it a sort of funeral polar."

"Montripier, you're a fool!... There's one objection that could be raised to my polar bear theory: the shape of the animal, so different from other bears."

"Ah, yes."

"It's not an objection. The polar bear's elongated form is due solely to its ichthyophagous diet."

At this, Cap struck such an attitude of triumph, that we

took his assertion as gospel, despite its less than obvious logic.

And we savored a *Rocky Mountain punch*[2], with an enormous amount of ice, to assure ourselves a vigorous old age.

Notes:

1. Cracked ice, a few drops of angostura, half a spoon of *crème de noyaux*, another of Curaçao, top off with brandy. Shake, strain, add lemon zest, drink.

2. Into a cobbler glass of crushed ice, add two teaspoons of sugar, the juice of half a lemon, half a glass of old rum, a tablespoon of Maraschino, and top it off with Saint-Marceaux, a piece of rock candy, and seasonal fruits. Drink with a straw.

Translator's Notes

Foreword: Louis Fouquet opened the Criterion Fouquet's Bar in 1899, at 99 Champs-Elysées; he later renamed it simply Fouquet's.

I: Fortunately, Andorra is landlocked.
La Lanterne was a satirical periodical edited by Henri Rochefort, and published 1868-1876. Allais added the question mark in the revision.
Curieux cas de sensibilité chez un requin ("Curious Case of Sensitivity in a Shark") can be found in Allais's earlier collection, *Rose et Vert-Pomme* (*Pink and Apple-Green*), 1894.

II: The Corrèze is a perfectly nice river in southwestern France.
Montmulot is a jocular term for Montmartre: Mount Mouse, rather than Mount Marten. One of Cap's campaign promises was to build an observatory there.

III: The good people of Gascony have a reputation for exaggeration.
Arthurville is a mere 23 miles from Quebec City.
Paul Fabre was indeed the son of the Canadian consul;

he also ran the Gardenia, the amateur theatrical society where Allais first met Cap. Maurice X. would be Maurice O'Reilly, a journalist who had also lived in Canada. Cap's membership in the Gardenia, coupled with a slight accent from his childhood in California, led some to think he was Canadian as well. Allais and Fabre visited Canada together in 1894; Allais particularly loved Quebec City, whose founders hailed from Honfleur.

IV: I found no source for the Source; the Pousset was a favorite writers' hangout.

The Faculty of Medicine in Nancy was known for research into hypnosis, led particularly by Hippolyte Bernheim.

Saucers were used to keep track of the bill. In another Allais story, *Moeurs de ce temps-ci* ("Manners Nowadays") a young bohemian is invited to dinner in a private home; after a few drinks, he collects all the saucers, saying, "This round is on me."

V: Antonin-Auguste Parmentier promoted potato cultivation in the 18th century.

VI: Poor Mr. Carnot indeed! Marie François Sadi Carnot, elected President of France in 1887, was assassinated in 1894.

Jean Moréas was responsible for the Symbolist Manifesto (1886).

Crème de noyaux is a liqueur made from apricot pits; I understand it's hard to find now.

Old Tom Gin, which recurs in many of the Captain's exploits, was sweeter than today's product.

VII: Many distillers seem to have made Anchor Gin.

One of the water purification plants in Auteuil still provides some water for Paris. The other now houses a museum.

The Barbotte is just a stream, really; Sorel is now known as Sorel-Tracy.

Cécile Sorel had a long career in the theater; she championed the traditional declamation of the Comédie-Française. A newsreel from 1933 shows her regally descending a staircase, then asking with magisterial coquetry, "Did I descend well?"

Albert Sorel was a historian; he was keen on Napoleon. His son wrote some novels, apparently.

In his horror at Schweppes, Cap quotes Luke 22:42.

Gum syrup, a simple syrup thickened with gum arabic, is also hard to find nowadays.

VIII: Mr. Pineau has left no trace; perhaps he really was a notary in Nice.

Cap actually discovers that Auguste's real name is
Charles, so that Allais can pun on "Charles l'orang" and
"Charles Laurent," then General Secretary of the Cabinet.
I substituted an equally odious anglophone pun for your
convenience.

IX: Allais's footnote about the eastern border refers, of
course, to Alsace-Lorraine, annexed by Germany in 1871.
"Let us always think it, but never say it," was a slogan
popularized by the statesman Léon Gambetta. Allais often
quoted it, sometimes, for variety, as "Let us always say it,
but never think it."

X: I'm afraid that the splendidly named Paul de
Gaultier de la Hupinière has gathered no moss. Perhaps
he was a friend or correspondent of Allais.

In the original version of the story, Allais himself was
the champion, and Mr. X. and Mr. Y. were portrayed by
Maurice O'Reilly and Captain Cap.

The School of Salerno was an early medical school,
particularly active from the 10th to the 13th centuries.

General Henri-Joseph Brugère had a long military career;
in 1900 he became the highest ranking officer in the
French army.

Jules-August Lemire was a noted priest, politician, and
reformer.

Charles Auguste Émile Durand, better known as Carolus

Duran, was a painter and teacher, specializing in portraits.

XI: Carl Auer von Welsbach first marketed his lamp (also known as the Welsbach mantle) in 1892; it soon became standard in streetlights.

Charles Cros was a close friend of Allais's; among other things, they experimented together with color photography. *"Études sur les moyens de communication avec les planètes"* ("Studies on methods of communication with other planets") was serialized in the journal *Le Cosmos* on August 7, 14, and 21, 1869; and then released as a booklet.

XII: Inspired by the prospect of an angler's cocktail, Allais quotes Verlaine. Or rather misquotes: the original line is "It weeps in my heart as it rains on the town." For some reason, he quotes it correctly in the original version of the story.

The Auteuil racetrack has long been a favorite subject for artists.

"After the rain, blue skies" is a traditional proverb. The Comtesse de Ségur used it as the title for a novel in 1871; I believe it ended happily.

XIII: Do I need to mention that Cap quotes François Villon when he invokes the snows of yesteryear? I may as well.

Mazagran is in the 10th arrondissement; however, it's a short street, with only 22 addresses.

XIV: Serquigny is indeed on the rail line, near Paris.

Émile Zurlinden was a general; Mikhail Ivanovich Dragomirov a Russian general; Félix Faure President of France; Félix Saussier another general.

XV: Jacques Callot produced many exquisite drawings, engravings, and etchings in the 17th century. Pierre Maël's output was perhaps more humdrum: under that name, Charles Vincent and Charles Causse published numerous patriotic and devotional children's books.

Yes, "bureaucratous": one of Allais's occasional neologisms.

Labitte de Montripier, I'm afraid, means "the penis of my tripe-dealer"; or, perhaps more idiomatically, "my butcher's wiener." Labitte is a fairly common surname, although many with the name have, understandably, changed it to Lafitte.

PART THREE
The Antifilter & Other Inventions

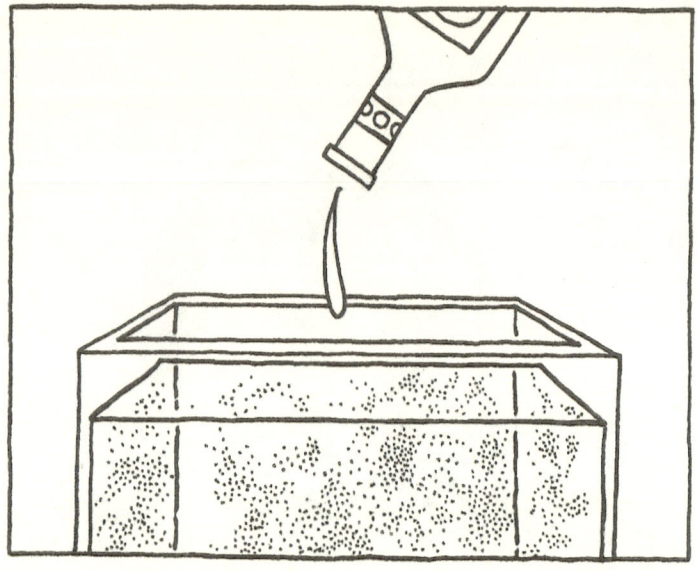

CHAPTER XVI

Captain Cap's antifilter, or a new way to give microbes what they deserve.

"Would it be indiscreet, my dear Cap, to ask you the contents of that parcel under your arm?"

"Not at all, my friend, not at all."

And, with a courtesy worthy of the age of chivalry, Cap unpacked his little parcel, and presented me with the contents: a cylindrical object, made of crystal and nickel, with rather mysterious hidden workings.

"What do you think this is?" interrogated Cap.

"A filter, similar to the Pasteur filter."

"Bravo!" cried Cap. "You guessed it! You guessed absolutely correctly, except for one minor detail: instead of a filter, this object is an antifilter."

A vivid yet mute astonishment overtook my features, and I was barely able to articulate: "An antifilter, Cap! An antifilter!"

"Yes," the Captain replied coldly, "an antifilter."

"Which is what?"

"My God, it's quite simple! Thanks to this apparatus, you can immediately transform the purest water into a yellowish fluid saturated with microbes. You see at once the advantages of my device."

"I see them, Cap, but can't quite distinguish them."

"Child that you are! Do you believe in antisepsis?"

"Certainly."

"And asepsis?"

"Certainly again!"

"Poor ninny! You're as bad as Major Heitner, who thinks water potable only when it's frozen, and then boiled in a pressure cooker, in the hope that all available microbes will die from heat and cold."

"Don't you mean cold and heat, Captain?"

"Why, that's true, I hadn't noticed. Major Heitner is even more inconsequential than I realized."

And to forget this unpleasant recognition of the major's excessive inconsequence, we entered, Cap and I, one of those little American bars which are the finest ornament of the Bay of Villefranche.

After ingesting a *lemon squash*[1], Cap continued:

"The stupid war that men wage on microbes will, sooner than later, cost humanity dearly."

"God save us, Cap!"

"We kill microbes, it's true, but we don't kill them all! And what do you call those that survive?"

"I don't call them, Cap, they come on their own."

"Ah, you don't call them! Well, I call them *nasty little buggers!* They're the ones who emerge from the trial more vigorous than ever, hardened for battle. In the fight for life, those individuals who aren't defeated gain a drive and a vigor that they pass on to their species. And soon, woe is us!"

"Let us kneel and pray, Cap!"

"Leave prayer to women and children. We men must stick to the truth. This is my theory about microbes: instead of fighting the little creatures, let us lull them into idleness and happiness. Let us offer them breeding grounds that are charming and favorable. May our bodies become a Capua for these microscopic Hannibals."

"That's a good one, Cap, *microscopic Hannibals!*"

"What will happen then? The microbes will become accustomed to this false security. They will multiply to their hearts' desire; but the more numerous they are, the less dangerous they are. Soon, they will decline into frank degeneracy."

"And Max Nordau will write a book about them. It will be quite enjoyable."

"So! What do you think of my theory?"

"Marvelous, Cap! Peace to all microbes of good will! And, to put your idea into practice, do microbes like *Irish cocktails?*"[2]

"They adore them, Alphonse, without a doubt!"

"So, waiter, two *gin cocktails!* And prepare them *carefully,* do you hear?"

"And *largefully,*" added Captain Cap with a smile.

If microbes do indeed adore American drinks, it was a good day for them, individually, but a deplorable one for their race.

Notes:

1. The *lemon squash* is the same as our lemonade: crushed ice, lemon juice, sugar, and seltzer or soda. Stir well, and add a slice of lemon.

2. The same recipe as the *brandy cocktail,* but replace the brandy with Old Tom Gin.

CHAPTER XVII

In which Captain Cap makes a successful ascension, without a craft, and with the regularity of a bird.

Captain Cap was beginning to bore me strangely, with his aerostats, flying and gliding machines, and the rest, all of which left me equally indifferent.

I was going to take my leave on some pretext, when a gentleman of robust appearance, who seemed to take a lively interest in Cap's extravagant ideas, arose and approached us. He offered his card, with the best manners in the world, a quite stylish card from the Stern company, upon which these words could be seen:

SIR O'GAYTE

Winnipeg

We are quite fond of Canada, Cap and I, and meeting a Canadian, even an English Canadian, always fills us with joy.

And so we welcomed, with pleasant mien, this noble foreigner, who graciously consented to accept a *champagne cobbler*.[1]

After we had exchanged the customary polite prelimi-
naries:

"It's just that," continued Sir O'Gayte, "when it comes
to aerostats, I know my stuff! I once ascended under conditions perhaps unique in the world!"

I saw Cap barely shrug his shoulders... *Conditions
unique in the world!* Foolish foreigner!

Unabashed, O'Gayte added:

"The peculiarity of my ascension is that the balloon was
myself."

Sir O'Gayte, after having had the courtesy to replenish
our glasses, said:

"It all happened about ten years ago... I was captain
of the brig *King of Feet,* loaded with sulfuric acid, and
headed for Hochelaga. One night, at the mouth of the St.
Lawrence, we were cut cleanly in two by a huge steamer,
from the *Dark-Blue Moon Line,* and we sank like a stone,
with all cargo and crew."

"Sad!"

"Quite sad, in fact! As for myself, I was wearing my
heavy leather *Bull-Shirt*: waterproof, if you please, but a
poor choice to challenge the record of any great swimmer.
I was nevertheless happy enough to be able to float for a
few moments, on a frail piece of wreckage. Finally, numb
with cold, I did as my ship and my little comrades had
done: I sank. But take notice: I didn't panic, and my plan
was already mapped out in my head."

"You're a cold-blooded one, aren't you?"

"I had plenty under the circumstances: it was late December."

"Very funny, sir!"

"With the heel of my boot, I stripped a shard of iron from the hull of the ship, and, having pulverized said shard with my muscular hands, swallowed it in one gulp. Gifted, in those days, with uncommon vigor, I then seized one of the carboys of sulfuric acid, and drank several mouthfuls."

"All this, at the bottom of the sea?"

"Yes sir, all this at the bottom of the sea! You can't always choose your laboratory. And you can guess what happened next, I suppose?"

"We can; but explain it anyway, for those of our readers who know Mr. Berthelot only by name."

"Quite right... When you combine iron, water, and an acid, hydrogen is released... I had only to hermetically close my natural orifices, particularly my mouth; after a few seconds, inflated with the precious gas, I regained the surface of the sea. But then!.. As it says in the ballad of the criminal Feynarou family, I had miscalculated the pressure. Not content just to float, I rose into the air, buoyed by a strong easterly wind that blew me over the river. This sport, new to me, at first enchanted, then monotonized me. At the break of day, I opened the corner of my lips slightly, like a gentleman who smiles. A bit of hydrogen leaked out; little by little, I returned to my normal weight, and soon set foot on solid ground, in a pretty little place called Tadoussac, at the mouth of the Saguenay. Do you know Tadoussac?"

"Do I know Tadoussac! And the pretty little old church! (the first that the French built in Canada). And the young ladies of Tadoussac, who sell photographs in the old little church to raise money for a new basilica!"

(And if these lines happen to fall under the eyes of the young ladies of Tadoussac, let them know that Messrs. P. F., E. D., B. de C., and A. A. cherish a memory that is both charming and indefeasible.)[2]

Once my parenthesis was closed, the gentleman from Winnipeg concluded his story, with an insouciance that was practically an insult to poor Cap:

"Once back on earth, I released the last bit of hydrogen from my luggage, and headed for the salmon farm in Tadoussac, lustily singing that old refrain that I love:

> Be it ever so humble,
> There's no play like horse.

Manifestly irritated, Cap shrugged his shoulders, muttering:

"He doesn't strike me as very serious."

Notes:

1. Fill a large glass with crushed ice, a teaspoon of Curaçao, another of *crème de noyaux,* and finish with that champagne that Saint-Marceaux makes. Stir, add a slice of orange, a slice of lemon, strawberries, and seasonal fruits. Shake, and then, without stirring, drizzle with port. Drink through a straw.

2. How long ago it was! And to think that those delectable damsels may now be enormous cows burdened with a thousand brats!

CHAPTER XVIII

*Description of an ingenious machine
invented by Cap to travel two hundred
and thirty-four kilometers an hour.*

Having met my excellent friend Captain Cap before the Leicester Tavern, I simply asked:

"Shall we enter?"

"No! Absolutely not!" Cap replied sharply.

"The Chicago Bar, then, which is nearby?"

"Neither the Chicago Bar nor the Leicester Tavern!"

"You worry me, Cap."

"As long as the Anglo-American conflict persists, I shall not set foot into a single John-Bullish or Uncle-Samian establishment![1] In my current position, strict neutrality is required."

"And what about Venezuelan brasseries, Cap, do you go to them?"

"As little as possible... Besides, I no longer drink in Paris. Whenever I feel thirsty, I head for the provinces. I straddle my nonuplet..."

"Pardon me for interrupting, Cap. Your... what do you straddle?"

"My nonuplet. Ah, you don't know about my nonuplet? As the name implies, it's a cycle mounted by nine people, just as a sextuplet is mounted by six."

"Nine people!"

"Ah, my nonuplet is a wonderful machine! Constructed entirely of wickerwork, assembled and reinforced by strips of gummed paper!"

"No metal!"

"Not a bit of metal! Not a bit!"

"And it's solid?"

"Why wouldn't it be, I ask you? A panther is solid! An albatross is solid! A shark is solid! And yet, show me a single metal part that went into the construction of any of those organisms! The Good Lord is too clever to use metal when He confects his little gadgets!"

"You must go fast, with your nonuplet?"

"Two hundred and thirty-four kilometers an hour."

"Cap, my dear old Cap! I'm afraid that you're taking advantage of my credulity."

"Not at all, my friend, I swear!"

"Two hundred and thirty-four kilometers an hour!"

"And not a millimeter less. I should add that my nonuplet, machine and riders combined, weighs a total of about a kilo."

"That explains everything, then. But a kilo, just think, a single kilo for all those people!"

"I should also add, to allay your doubts, that my nonuplet is lightened by a balloon, whose ascensional force is equal, give or take a kilo, to the weight of the machine and its riders."

"You don't say! But what about the wind resistance against the balloon?"

"There is none! My balloon is shaped like a double-pointed corkscrew, with one point in front, and the other in back. It twists through the air just as a corkscrew screws through cork, that is, with no appreciable resistance. Wherever the wind may blow, it can't make us so much as shrug our shoulders."

"Poor wind!"

"And so, my dear Allais, make up your mind! Come have a drink with us in Dunkirk!"

"With pleasure!"

My acceptance seemed to delight Cap, but he remembered that he had suffered a slight accident, that very morning, to one of the willow strips in his nonuplet. And so we went into a little gold and white cafe, where a middle-aged waiter served us two excellent mugs of Tourtel beer.

Notes:

1. These adventures unfolded in an epoch in which England and the United States were divided by such a serious conflict that nobody today can remember what it was about.

> ## CHAPTER XIX
> *What one might call, without hesitation,*
> *a truly modern house.*

"Well, my old Cap, what do you think of this?"

"Of what?"

I handed Cap the issue of the *Journal* in which Marcel Prévost expounded, with his usual authority and charm, the subject of the modern house.[1]

With a rapid glance, one of those rapid glances that the most perspicacious eagle would not have hesitated to sign, our valiant comrade had soon devoured the article.

Then he shrugged, and, with that attitude that is his alone, said:

"Your friend Prévost seems quite naive, to become so exercised over an elevator for the garbage, and for a heated bathroom."

"Have you seen better, Cap?"

"Child!"

"In New South Wales, I suppose?"

"Not that far away; in northern Canada, in Winnipeg, I

saw a house that was constructed perfectly for the climate, which is glacial in winter, and torrid in summer."

"Radiators? Ventilators?"

"Better than that! I'm talking about an apartment house that, in the rough season, is always exposed to the south."

"Ah, my old Cap! I won't fall for that one again, I've already heard it!"

"Heard what?"

"In San Remo, there is a hotel which, among other enticements, prints this curious notice in its brochure: *Thanks to an ingenious arrangement, all rooms in the hotel face south.*[2] Well, this is the ingenious arrangement: the building is quite thin, only one room wide; which means, of course, that all rooms face the same way, south. And that's what you call an ideal house."

"When you stop talking, I'll continue."

"Go on."

"Like your hotel in San Remo, my house in Winnipeg is rather narrow, being only two rooms wide, but what makes it unique is that it sits upon an enormous wagon, which turns on a circular track."

"I'm beginning to understand."

"My house is a turning house. In the front are the master bedrooms, dining rooms, parlors, etc.; in the rear, the kitchens, servants' quarters, dens for mothers-in-law, etc. During the winter, a season in which the weakest sunbeam is a blessing, my house, exposed to the sunrise in the morning, turns until evening, when it points toward the sunset, only to begin anew the next day."

"Quite ingenious."

"During the summer, the torrid summer of those latitudes, it turns in the opposite direction, so that one can flee the horrors of the blistering noon."

"Admirable!"

"We are a long way, are we not, my friend, from Marcel Prévost's modern house, with its enamel pipes to keep microbes out of the apartment!"

...

"A bit of *coffee punch*[3], Captain?"

"With pleasure!" said Cap.

Notes:

1. How long ago it was.

2. True.

3. Into a glass of crushed ice, add a half teaspoon of *crème de noyaux;* fill half the glass with Curaçao, add two teaspoons of sugar, a jigger of cognac, another of rum, and one of kirsch. Top off with good black coffee, shake, strain, and drink with a straw.

CHAPTER XX

A creation of Captain Cap's:
the Grandiose Billiards Club!

It looked as if the rain had not decided not to fall, so I proposed to Captain Cap that we play a game of billiards, simply, I added, to kill time.

"Alas!" Cap replied, "it is not we who kill time, but time that kills us!"

"Just to make it pass, then."

"Alas!" Cap repeated, "it is not we who make time pass, but time that makes us pass."

We could have continued quite a while with this system, so I thought it best not to insist.

But I insisted anyway.

"With pleasure," the hardy navigator agreed, "but where?"

"Right here, Cap, on the second floor."

(For I should inform the reader, if there is still time, that the scene took place in the little white cafe on Blue Street—far preferable, in my opinion, to the little blue cafe on White Street.)

Cap merely shrugged.

"Billiards on the second floor! You jest, my friend!"

"I..."

"A billiard table that can fit into a city building, as vast as that city building may be, is nothing but a contemptible plaything, fit only for little boys and girls."

"Ah!"

"The last time that I played billiards, as you see me now, my dear Alphonse, was in New South Wales."

"Ah!"

"And on a table whose shorter side measured no less than one and a half marine miles (2 km 787 m)."

"Good heavens, my friend!"

And my stupefaction, I admit, was tempered with a dash of incredulity.

"Precisely," Cap said in his quietest tone.

And when that devil of a man had told me his story, I realized—Good Lord! that the monstrosity of his claim was purely illusory.

...In 1888[1], Cap, sent by the Free Institute of Bougival on a geological survey in New South Wales, had ventured into the bottom of a wide valley, where the hand of man had never set foot.

No vegetation flourished there, for the excellent reason that the soil had been replaced by a formidable layer of malachite.

Contrary to the old proverb, which states that sheet ores never prosper[2], Cap put this mineralogical treasure to extraordinarily good use.

In no time at all, he had leveled the block of malachite horizontally, and founded in Pifpaftown (the nearest city to the site) the *Grandiose Billiards Club.*

Just to cushion the sides of the mammoth table took more than six thousand quintals of rubber. The balls—an ingenious innovation—were enormous spheres of Dutch cheese, which a rather simple process (using aluminum pyrolignite) had rendered into ivory of the highest quality. Of course, with such a gigantic arrangement, one could not even think of using cues, like you or I.

Cannons, mounted on cable-cars of the latest design, rolled upon a track encircling the exorbitant table, and fired the enormous balls onto the surface of the malachite.

The player's skill, then, lay not only in correct aim, but in calculating the proper amount of powder to load into the cartridge.

Cap assured me that the sport quickly became addictive.

And I was no longer surprised at his contempt for our poor little pathetic European billiards.

Notes:

1. How long ago it was!

2. Please pronounce "sheet ores" quickly, or my joke will lose much of its savor.

CHAPTER XXI

In which Captain Cap gives us some interesting insights into the shoeing of horses on the Australian pampas.

"And you, Cap? What do you think of all that?"

"All that... what?"

"All that, all that..."

"Ah, yes! All that! Well, I think one thing, and one thing only!"

"Which is?"

"Oh, nothing."

Our conversation continued awhile in this vein. I felt a bit depressed, while the usually vivacious Captain Cap seemed totally exhausted.

Cap yawned, stretched like a big sleepy cat, and I could tell at once what he would suggest: the inevitable *cosmopolitan claret punch*[1] in some nearby Saxon bar. I responded with two curtly uttered monosyllables:

"No, Cap."

Had all of Mount Valerian, tossed by an expert hand, landed on his head, Cap could not have been more formally annihilated.

"What," he stammered, "did you say?"

"I said: *No, Cap.*"

"But I don't understand."

"It's quite simple, Cap. Henceforth, debauchery, in whatever form it may present itself, fills me with unspeakable horror. I have found my road to Damascus. No more excess! Moderation for me! Let us live with nature! And nature needs no fermented or spiritous beverages. If we had not created alcohol, my dear Captain, we would not have had to invent cold showers."

I felt truly sorry for Cap. Such ideas upset him so, especially spoken by his old companion in debauch.

In desperation, he suspected a joke.

"No, Cap, seriously!" I insisted.

Poor Cap!

I saw that he had the sensation—the horrible, cold, dark sensation—that he was losing a comrade.

Don't fret, Cap! You may lose a companion, but the friend remains; for I knew to look through the apparently inextricable barrier of your exterior, to the heart of pure gold that shudders within.

Timidly, Cap asked:

"Are you doing anything this afternoon?"

"Nothing until six."

"What do you say we take a little trip to the inn in Celle-Saint-Cloud?"

"Why not?"

Cap and I have a long history with that inn.

How many times has the light clear wine that we decanted there settled so cheerfully the redoubtable American drinks of the night before!

It was a cold dry day, perfect for a trip into the country west of Paris.

Our little Comiot motorcycle rolled jauntily down the road.

We had hardly passed the city limits, when, in the course of who knows what discussion, Cap felt it necessary to compare his throat to a rasp, a veritable rasp.

I took pity.

The tavern where we stopped was next to a blacksmith.

The smell of burned hooves wafted to our nostrils, and the din of anvils assailed our ears.

It had been far too long since Cap had inveighed against Europe. I let him speak:

"You really have to come to this filthy country to see horses shod so absurdly."

"Do you know another way, Cap?"

"Another way?... A thousand other ways, all more effective, more practical, and more elegant."

"Such as?"

"Such as, the method used on the prairies of central Australia, when wild horses must be shod, horses so wild they cannot be approached."

"You've seen horses shod at a distance?"

"My poor friend, it's child's play for the people there!"

"Not that I'm curious, but..."

"And yet nothing could be less complicated. The black-smiths of that country use a small quick-firing cannon, much like the Canet cannon (which our navy should hasten to adopt, between parentheses). Instead of shells, the arms are loaded with horseshoes, complete with nails. With a bit of training, some practice, and a sure eye, it's as easy as pie. You wait until the horse gallops into range and shows its heels, if you will excuse the expression... At that moment, bang bang bang bang! You shoot off four times, if you will again excuse the expression, and the irons are nailed to the courser's hooves. Your mustang is shod! After that, the poor animal is so perplexed, that you can approach it as easily as a roast lamb broaches the green beans."

"Marvelous!"

"Isn't it? But, heavens! It does take skill."

At that moment, the innkeeper's maid entered with a pot of fine creamy milk, freshly drawn.

"Say," said Cap, "why don't we make an *ice cream soda?*"

And to the great amazement of the suburbanites, Cap prepared us one of the most delicious *ice cream sodas*[2] I have ever tasted.

Notes:

1. In a large glass of crushed ice, add a teaspoon of raspberry syrup, one of Maraschino, one of Curaçao. Add a jigger of brandy, finish with aged Bordeaux. A slice of orange, seasonal fruits, a straw.

2. Cap proceeds in this way: into a receptacle filled with ice that he has crushed himself, he adds two jiggers of vanilla liqueur and one of kirsch. He fills the rest with one part milk and one part seltzer. You can vary it to taste by replacing the vanilla with cocoa, or whatever liqueur you prefer. You can also substitute rum for the kirsch.

CHAPTER XXII

*In which Captain Cap plays a trick—
and quite a trick, at that—on the
estimable Mr. Alphonse Allais.*

It will be a long time before I pardon that shameless prankster Cap for the atrocious—yes, atrocious!—joke that he played at my expense.

When he puts his mind to it, Cap earns his title of Captain; and, once he gets you aboard, can easily take you around the bend.

A few weeks ago, a gentleman that we met in the course of some debauch, and with whom we at once forged the bonds of an inoxydizable friendship, warmly entreated us:

"Above all, if you ever make it to Touraine, you mustn't leave without staying a few days with me, in B. I will give you such a little Vouvray! Such a little Bourgeuil! Such a little Chinon! Such a little Saint-Avertin!"

Four significant smacking of the lips punctuated these enticements.

"It will be a change," he added, "from your infernal *whiskey cocktails.*" [1]

I had long forgotten our friendly invitation from Mr. Peeplehier (for that was his name), when, one fine morning, Cap suggested:

"You know what? We really should go do a little wine tasting with our friend from a few days ago."

"There's an idea! Waiter, the train schedule!"

.....

It was only at the station in B. that we realized that Peeplehier's exact address was missing from our notebook.

"Bah!" said Cap. "The first bus driver that we see will tell us. A man like him must be popular in his own town."

In fact, the first driver that we saw did tell Cap, and told Cap with seven or eight words at the most, but which were enough to enlighten Cap.

I must emphasize this point.

I didn't hear the driver's response, but, given the infinitesimal duration of the conversation, I could, without fear of exaggeration, estimate said response at seven or eight words—let's say ten, to be generous.

Cap told me: "I know where it is. Follow me."

.....

Like many little towns on the Orleans line, B. has a station located in a suburb, far from the true urban agglomeration, from which it is separated by a long avenue lined with lindens.[2]

Dating back to the time of François I, if not earlier, this historic city offers to the enchanted traveler an inextricable web of little streets, admittedly picturesque, but highly labyrinthous.

The amazing thing is that the damned Captain made his way through the maze, as easily and freely as he might have strolled through Chicago, Quebec, or any of his other native cities.

There are two possibilities, I thought: either Cap had been here before, although I was certain of the contrary; or he was walking along blindly, at the risk of getting us hopelessly lost.

From time to time, like a prophet consulting birds in the sky, Cap raised an inspired eye to the firmament, then:

"We take a left," he announced decisively.

"Are you sure?... I'm starting to get tired, you know."

And my friend simply shrugged.

Then, soon after:

"Do you see that big brick house?" he said, extending a triumphant hand. "Well, that's it."

And it was!

. . . . .

How the devil could he find his way, given such brief and furtive directions from the driver (ten words, I later learned), with such precision, through an infinitely complicated city in which he had never set foot, to a building that he indicated in advance, although he had never seen it before?

. . . . .

Peeplehier received us royally, but I couldn't sleep a wink all night, tormented as I was by the irritating enigma, about which Cap merely said:

"I have an unusually developed sense of direction. That's all."

Enhanced perhaps by excessive consumption of the principal Tourangian vintages at dinner, my agitation knew no bounds.

Ten times, twenty times, during the meal, I implored Cap:

"You see in what a nervous state—ridiculous, I admit, but all too real—you've put me with your refusal to explain. This is not the act of a friend."

"But," Cap coldly repeated, "I already told you! There's nothing out of the ordinary about this little event. I'm gifted with an exceptionally keen sense of direction!"

Impossible to get another word from him!

Our gracious host, Mr. Peeplehier, fared no better in his attempt to cast a light on this curious mystery.

Toward midnight, when we parted for our separate rooms, I had the idea, fearing that the next day I might, in my distress, imagine that it was all a hallucination provoked by too much Vouvray, I had the idea, I say, to compose a sort of brief on the adventure that so preoccupied me, and I wrote:

"Today, invited to spend a few days with Mr. Peeplehier, my friend Cap and I arrived in B., a small town in which (I am sure) neither Cap nor I had ever set foot.

"Not knowing our host's address, Cap asked directions from a bus driver parked in the courtyard by the station.

"This last supplied Cap with the requested information, but in such a summary fashion that the entire exchange lasted no more than ten seconds.

"Despite these necessarily rudimentary directions, despite the distance to the domicile in question, despite the virtually inextricable complication of the little streets and alleys of the city of B., Cap led me directly, without a hint of error or hesitation, to Mr. Peeplehier.

"Even better, as we turned into the street where the gentleman lived, Cap pointed to a building some fifty meters away, saying, 'You see that big brick house? That's where our friend lives.'

"Cap was not mistaken.

"Diabolically delighted to see me so mystified, Cap refuses the slightest explanation.

"If tomorrow I receive no solution to the riddle, I am perfectly prepared to kill Cap, and to then perish, if necessary, on the scaffold."

.....

The next morning, still tormented by my intolerable obsession, I arose before everybody else and headed for the station.

I had an idea.

Just then, a bus arrived, driven by the man whom we had consulted the day before.

"Excuse me, my good fellow, could you direct me to Mr. Peeplehier?"

"Peeplehier? The big brick house next to the post office..."

"Not another word, my good fellow, thank you! Here's twenty sous for your trouble."

I took a deep breath.

I was relieved.

The solution to the puzzle had come to me in a flash!

How stupid of me, all the same, to work myself up into such a state, when the key to the mystery was so simple!

When, during our walk the other day, Cap looked to the sky, like a prophet consulting the flight of the birds, it was just to check the direction of the telegraph wires leading from the railway to the post office in B.

It was no more complicated than that!

But the day that the wireless telegraph is officially adopted, my practical joker friend Cap will have to come up with something else.

Notes:

1. Put into your cocktail shaker a few pieces of ice, a few drops of angostura, a small amount of Curaçao and *crème de noyaux*, and complete with scotch. Shake, strain, and pour. When the cocktail is served, cut a lemon rind carefully into thin strips, bruise them to release the oil, and add them to your glass.

2. In some other cities, the lindens are replaced by plane-trees. Different people have different customs.

CHAPTER XXIII

In which Mr. Mougeot's mercantile cynicism offends the delicate soul of Captain Cap.

An old administrative custom demands that, every year, the Director General of the French Post Office apply all of his care, and all of his taste, to the creation of a splendid and deluxe calendar, printed in a limited edition; and that he take the trouble, this high official, to present copies to the Chief of State, the Minister, the Presidents of the Chambers, and, finally, to a few of the more notable personalities who so rightfully honor our homeland.

So it was, that one fine morning in late December, Captain Cap received a visit from Mr. Mougeot.[1]

No matter, my dear friends, how confident you may be of your own worth, such a call cannot but move you deeply, especially when you have done nothing to invite it; and Cap was at a loss how to thank our active Under Secretary of State for his thousand times too flattering, as he put it, graciousness.

But then it was up to his visitor to protest, and to pour out such praise, and such compliments, and such exultations, that it finally turned that shrinking violet that is the

Captain into the most embarrassed of poppies.

(A violet changed into a poppy! A curious case of transformism! What do you think of that, ghost of old Darwin?)

When they had exhausted the gamut, Mr. Mougeot of eulogy, and Cap of gratitude, the latter thought to take a look at the marvelous object he had been given.

Yes, I said "marvelous," and will not retract the word, for never before has our national industry, never before has the exquisite taste of our artisans produced anything quite so delectable.

Examining his calendar more closely, suddenly, Cap could not suppress an exclamation of surprise!

He had made a bizarre discovery: the saints for every day had been eliminated, and replaced...

You will never guess!

Replaced by the names of those commercial, industrial, and hygienic products whose merits you see touted in newspapers, on posters, and, in a word, everywhere that the human eye can exercise its vision.

For example, instead of that old reference we have known since childhood: "January 4, Friday, Saint Rigobert," we see, and not without surprise, "January 4, Friday, Menier Chocolate."

And on Tuesday, April 16, poor Saint Fructuosus is blithely replaced by "Simon Cream"!

And so on for the rest, up to December 31, where Saint

Sylvester is dethroned by... *The Twentieth Century Watch.*

.....

Mr. Mougeot smiled.

"Yes, my friend, this is our new almanac; the one in your hands is but an opulent sample."

"Strange!"

"Only at first. The people of France, my dear sir, get used to everything; and this innovation will be even more acceptable when they realize that it will bring a few tidy millions into the treasury."

"Yes, but tradition... Aren't you afraid?"

"Men like me, my friend, with one hand grasping the shoulder of progress, and the other crushing the hydra of tradition beneath its heel, fear nothing,"

"Congratulations!"

"As soon as the budget is balanced, I will introduce a bill granting the state a monopoly on the publication and sale of calendars. The government already sells stamps, tobacco, matches, etc.; there's nothing extraordinary in the idea that it become a dealer in almanacs."

"True."

"And you can guess the rest... Ah yes! Money first!"

When he told me this story, Cap concluded with a sigh:

"How France has changed since the Crusades!"

And as a sudden chill had made the conversation even sadder, we immediately fell upon a particularly comforting *gin cling*.[2]

Notes:

1. The reader is intelligent enough to understand on his, or her, own that Mr. Mougeot was then at the head of the well known administration devoted to the mail and the telegraph.

2. To obtain a *gin cling*, heat one part gin and one part water, add sugar and lemon, then pour and drink before it cools.

CHAPTER XXIV

In which we see our friend Captain Cap, like Saint Michael vanquishing the demon, get the better of the coldest temperatures.

The phenomenon generally designated under the name of "cold" results, nine times out of ten, from the temperature.

Remove the cause, and you remove the effect; raise a lower temperature, and you will be astonished to see the cold disappear.

It is probably for this reason that we have the ancient custom, as old as the world, of starting a fire for warmth.

Nothing is easier than starting a fire, but nothing— alas!—as expensive.

And I think you will agree that the more humanity progresses, the more the price of fuel will rise to the dizziest heights of the vertiginous. Ah! For those who are cold, the future is painted in dark colors indeed. (If only it were dark red!)

Does this mean that the situation is hopeless?

No. But from now on, my dear friends, we must no longer play the fool; we must abandon our old and barbarous system of furnaces that burn wood, charcoal, coal, etc., etc.

In a word, in this field, as in all others on which the thousand problems of life depend, we must resolve, once and for all, to show that we are scientific, and, far removed from the traditions of our ancestors, but resolutely within the firmament of true modern civilization, seek the torch that will guide us, I cannot say to perfect happiness, for perfect happiness is not of this world, as So-and-So rightly states, but quite modestly, and this will be even lovelier, don't you think?, toward the comfortable. Whew!

But enough preamble. To the facts!

.....

It was night; and we found ourselves, Captain Cap and I, alone in a car on the Western line, when a conscientious employee entered to change our hot-water bottles.

Unfortunately, due either to a thrifty management, or to personal error, he exchanged our two one-eyed bottles for two blind ones, that is to say, and I believe I'm right about this, he inflicted upon us two from the next car, while the next car benefitted from ours (as is done in the best homes).

I confined myself to a shrug of the shoulders (constrained as I am by my benefits from the Western Company); but my companion flew into a towering rage, and showered the station's personnel with an opaque flock of assorted insults.

Then, turning to me:

"And to think," he cried, "that nothing will change until

my system is adopted!"

"Your system, Cap?"

Do you like people with systems? Nothing is more agreeable on a long voyage!

As with almost all brilliant inventions, chance played a large part in the discovery that concerns us here.

Perhaps not chance, really, but circumstance, to be more precise.

Cap[1] fulfilled his military service in some garrison, I forget which, in the mountains, known for its extreme frigidity.

One night when he was on sentry duty outside the magazine, and had forgotten his gloves, a wild terror seized him: his two hands, his two poor hands, suddenly began to swell visibly, if you will excuse the expression, and—there could be no doubt!—those appendages, so useful to man, were about to freeze to the bone.

A horrible situation!

Frozen hands!

And the poor boy, quickly dropping his rifle, blew on his fingers, clapped his hands together, crammed them into his pockets, and into the most intimate folds of his clothing.

Nothing worked: his hands, he realized with frightening clarity, were taking great strides along the path of definitive freezing.

It was then that he had a stroke of genius!

Seizing his firearm, without hesitation he fired into the darkness, and shot off, one by one, half a dozen rounds.

After which, holding his hands to the smoking barrel of his Lebel, he felt his circulation return: he was saved!

It is this procedure that Cap calls "his system," and which he seeks, in vain, to have adopted by the railways and other concerns. But routine, always that damned routine!

Notes:

1. Before devoting himself to the navy, Cap insisted on serving several years in the terrestrial army, so that he might see first hand, as he claims, the many abuses that teem there.

CHAPTER XXV

*In which it is a question, it must be said,
of a lot of nastiness.*

An excellent Christmas Eve, spent with a few hetaerae of exceptional beauty, and five or six prevaricating deputies, all under the scintillating direction of Captain Cap.

That devil of a man loses no opportunity to instruct as he entertains. Let us, then, give him the floor:

The custom of eating sausages on Christmas Eve is of great antiquity.

Don't we read in Caesar's *Commentaries: Secundum antiquum habitudinem Lexoviani celebrant birthiae Christi stuffandos e ipsos cum boldini* [1] *fantasticis quantitatibus?*

If we leave the domain of history for the greater precision of statistics, we can embellish our brains with the following numbers:

One hundred average French citizens (for we cannot, of course, include very young children, many moribunds, women in childbirth, and certain personalities such as Mr. Paul Deschanel, too refined to ever admit the ingestion of such vulgar foodstuffs), one hundred average French citizens, I say, consume one meter of sausages.[2] One meter of sausages for every hundred inhabitants represents, if I can count (and I can, I assure you), some thirty-odd kilometers for all of France.

If you will be so kind, ladies and gentlemen, please note this figure on a scrap of paper; we will return to it soon.

...And now, if you are willing, we will leave statistics to leap into the field of what we will call, for lack of a better word, biology.

In its last issue, the excellent *Journal of Medicine and Surgery*, ably edited by Dr. Lucas-Champonnière, summarized, from an uncredited German publication, a rather unappetizing account of the research of a certain Dr. Schelling.

Having probably nothing to do between meals, this scholar succeeded—not without some difficulty, he claims—in procuring fresh intestines, such as butchers use to prepare sausages, chitterlings, frankfurters, and other delicacies, "*ejusdem offaliae.*"

He examined them, these intestines, with powerful microscopes; he scrutinized their hidden folds; he scratched them; he analyzed the scrapings, and finally discovered...

(Those with sensitive stomachs, and who intend to use any of the products mentioned above, are urged immediately to read no further.)

He discovered, our excellent Dr. Schelling, that the intestines used to form those succulent sausages and appetizing frankfurters contain a quantity of excrement, amounting to two or two and a half grams per meter for the small intestine, and five grams per meter for the large intestine.

Please note that the intestines that Dr. Schelling investigated came from a butcher renowned in the area for his meticulous cleanliness.

"A German worker," Dr. Schelling adds sadly, "who consumes ten to fifteen centimeters of sausage a day, an ordinary average, ingests four or five grams of excrement a week, or a half pound a year."

Do you remember an old play, quite amusing, called *The Shit Peddler*?

An admittedly offensive title, which could now be changed to another, more hypocritical perhaps, but with the same meaning: *The Butcher.*

...Let us return then to our sausages, to our thirty kilometers of sausages, and conclude that on Christmas Eve, as we gather together, one hundred and fifty kilos of... the merchandise in question will be eaten within the territory of the French republic.

A deplorable finding; for, after all, there is no reason, just because Christ was born in a stable, to gorge ourselves tonight on cow dung.

Notes:

1. This has nothing to do with the celebrated painter; it's not my fault if the Latin word for sausage is *baldinum*.

2. Contrary to Captain Cap's usual praxis, these statistics are on the low side.

CHAPTER XXVI

In which we see clouds of hail defeated by Captain Cap's system. The Captain's theory on the formation of coal.

Hail—and Émile Gautier will second me on this—is a sort of conglomerate formed of frozen water.

Falling from a high altitude, cravenly abusing the law of falling bodies, each hailstone becomes a sort of miniature Attila, welcomed only by glaziers, destroying all hopes of crops and harvests, and—for the villain stops at nothing—often the crops and harvests themselves.

"Hailo farmeribus detestata!"

Humanity long remained helpless before this witless aggression.

Then came companies that offered insurance against hail.

But that only dodges the problem, and, as far as I'm concerned, makes it worse.

To demand a hundred sous from farmers when they have a good crop, only to reimburse them fifty centimes on the day that it's destroyed: if you call that progress, you are none too particular.

Yes, you are none too particular!

You are so unparticular that I prefer to draw a veil over such activities, and to turn resolutely to the subject of artillery, so that we can be done sooner.

Émile Gautier, whom I quoted above, discoursed a few days ago on the pros and cons of setting off explosives against hail.

Eventually, and, incidentally, in accordance with many studies done over the years, Gautier decided in favor of the efficacious cannon.

Henceforth, whenever we see a shifty cloud that looks about to hail, we will riddle it with bullets, and rain will replace the destructive hailstone.

The theory then can be comprised in these three words (three little words): "Disturb clouds by shooting them with cannons!"

The only drawback to this seductive system is that it requires munitions, powder, special gunners—in a word, all of God's thunder, or rather Man's!

What an expense for a small town, and what a lot of trouble!

.....

Solicited by many enterprises—agricultural, vinicultural, and others ending in "cultural"—to simplify the procedure, and to obtain better results with less "fuss," Captain Cap felt his shoulders shrug of their own accord at the easiness of the task.

Would it not be—and he will let you be the judge—simpler, when disturbing the clouds, to disturb them in their own nest, thanks to rustic balloons, made of paper, each carrying a pound of sporting powder lit by a simple fuse, like those that our pyrotechnists use to ignite impressive fireworks from afar, on the evening of July 14th, to a thousand cries of "Long live the Republic!"

Quite simple, really, but—we must keep repeating—you have to think of it first.

As was observed, and quite judiciously, yesterday by the charming countess Ouateva, the price of coal is going through the roof.

Let us be men, and not shirk the atrocious truth: an industrial crisis is in the offing.

The question of coal, ladies and gentlemen... But before we get to the crux of the problem, let us call upon the excellent research of Captain Cap, to correct any false ideas our readers may have on the formation of coal.

Let us be done with the silly legend that coal mines were produced by huge forests, consumed by fire and buried deep underground, millions of years ago, when the surface of our globe consisted of universal swampland.

How can we, in fact, find this hypothesis tenable, that, the earth being in that antediluvian era so prodigiously aquatic, entire forests could have caught on fire and been entirely destroyed, without everything else that populated the world following that burning example?

The old theory will not stand.

Captain Cap's theory seems better suited for anyone smitten with verisimilitude and common sense: that is, the overwhelming majority of our clear-sighted readers.

We know that if we erect certain buildings, we must, given the poor condition of some marshy or sandy terrain, indulge in that operation specialists call "pile-driving."

It appears obvious that all buildings from that era were constructed on pilings.

(Let us add that to drive in those innumerable piles, primitive men, our joyous ancestors, in their ignorance of current technology, trained beavers for the task; and that the aptitude, still seen today among our rare contemporary beavers, for hammering in chimerical stakes, is simply a hereditary acquisition.)

Why not admit, then, that all of the coal that we now find in our basements comes from this formidable subterranean reserve?

Why not, after all?

CHAPTER XXVII

The difficulty of poetry for certain foreigners.

"Cap, you touch upon all of the sciences, and all of the arts, with equal mastery, so how is it that I've never heard your poetry?"

"I wrote verses, my friend, when I was young; I wrote enough to fill cotton warehouses and grain silos. When I decided to burn them, I was in Melbourne, and the sky was black for over a week."

"Fool!"

And Cap burst into laughter.

"Do you know," he added, "my friend Tom Otto?"

"No."

"Well then, listen to this little story about a foreign poet."

A few weeks ago, when I was in London, there disembarked, bearing a letter of introduction addressed to myself, a young Dutchman from Appeldoorn named Tom Otto, an appellation fully justified by the bright red of his capillary system.

But it was not due to his scarlet hair that young Tom Otto attracted the attention of the connoisseur; it was rather his capricious way of pronouncing the beautiful English language, a way so capricious, that the ear most experienced in Dutch gutturals could not have found in his conversation the least discernible iota.

In fact, many superficial minds, on hearing my young friend, even swore that he spoke some dialect from Gabon.

It must be added in his defense that, in the deepest recesses of the Lowlands, entirely bereft of the smallest English companion, Tom Otto, by will power alone—ah, the discipline of those Northerners!—succeeded in learning English, on his own, with a few books from a second-hand shop.

In the simplicity of his soul, fortified with this ad hoc education, Tom Otto settled the question of pronunciation by ignoring it, and pronounced English as he had pronounced the language of Rembrandt since birth.

So that, since his arrival in England, he had met nobody, with the exception of one individual, with whom he could converse, without difficulty, in their language.

And you should have seen them—and not heard them, as you will understand in a moment—chewing the interminable fat, my friend Tom Otto and a certain Loudon Cleere, a young deaf-mute from Glasgow whom our Dutchman met at a concert!

The silent Loudon Cleere—ironic name!—placed no importance on pronunciation. And since his disability saved the poor Scot the inconvenience of a Glaswegian burr, Tom and Loudon experienced no difficulty in understanding one another, and the two fine lads communicated perfectly—by gestures, of course.

Loudon Cleere even came to have a great influence over Tom Otto, and soon convinced him to start writing poetry, as he himself had done since childhood.

Except that, my goodness, Loudon did come up with some peculiar rhymes.

Not satisfied with coupling those golden rhymes, he tripled them.

(I don't mean to imply that Loudon invented the technique—others have used it as well—but he did apply it with unusual rigor.)

Soon afterward, Tom Otto brought me a little poem that opened with this curious tercet:

> The bush was very close,
> And so I picked a rose,
> To give to my friend José,
> Etc., etc.

"But, my poor friend," I could not help exclaiming, "it doesn't rhyme!"

"I know that," Tom replied, "Loudon told me."

"How would he know, being deaf?"

"He could see it with his eyes, my friend. He reproached me for the accent on the last word."

"He was right."

"Well, I'll begin again, that's all! Until tomorrow!"

And the next day, in fact, Tom Otto submitted for my approval a second piece, of great eloquence, of profound philosophy, but which began like this:

> One day I found a stone;
> The next day it was gone,
> And I was left with none.
> Etc., etc.

Before such good intentions—what can I tell you?—I could only bow.

"This time, old man, you've got it! Congratulations."

And embarrassment, then, turned Tom Otto's face as red as his hair.

CHAPTER XXVIII

An odious violation of a formal rule.

In Captain Cap's mail this morning was the following letter, which he entrusted to me, since its publication could save millions of human beings, not to mention animals (for nothing prevents them from being in the same circumstance) from one of the most horrible deaths that it has been given the inhabitants of our planet to undergo:

"Dear sir and illustrious Captain,

"I do not have the honor of your acquaintance, but one of my colleagues in the office indicated you to me as one of the rare individuals alive today who has not sold out to one of our large administrations.

"You are therefore admirably suited, dear sir, to inform the public about one of the most incredible administrative monstrosities which, and I might add, for over fifty years, it has had to suffer.

"To suffer, I said? To die!

"...When, dear sir and illustrious Captain, we introduced into France that mode of public transportation called the railroad, our legislators, as was their duty, did not neglect to surround the new institution with a host of administrative precautions, assuring travelers of all possible guarantees against the thousand accidents that this method of locomotion might incur.

"Of these regulations, some have been enforced since the beginning, and have not ceased, and will not cease, to be.

"Those regulations, I need not emphasize, are the ones that do not overly trouble the Company's employees, and that make only insignificant demands on the capital of those gentlemen, the shareholders.

"The others have remained a dead letter.

"We need not be surprised, then, at the number of railway catastrophes in the daily press!

"Would you like an example, a simple example that says more than the most violent diatribe?

"Then procure for yourself the Ordinance bearing the title:

"*Ordinance establishing public administrative regulations for the policing, security, and exploitation of the railways.*

"Let us pass over a number of nevertheless interesting details about which there would be much to say, and stop at *title VIII, article 73*.

"I quote verbatim:

"'Every agent employed on the railway will wear a uniform or carry a distinctive sign; the roadmen, gate-keepers, and supervisors may also be armed with a saber.'

"Now, tell me honestly, have you ever seen even one railway employee, from the humble roadman to the dis-tinguished president of the administrative council, wear a saber?

"I can predict the objection from the mild-mannered taxpayer, ready to think that all is well: if agents were in-deed armed with sabers, could they use those implements to prevent derailments, collisions, telescopings, and other foolishness?

"Obviously not, but there is more to the question.

"Our legislators, by authorizing the wearing of sabers, but not rapiers, by certain railway agents, clearly intended those agents to be mounted.

"After all, does it not stand to reason that an official on horseback can accomplish far more serious duties than one on foot?

"But for the sake of miserly economy, of hideous rapac-ity, of nauseating lucre, the railway has never dreamed—never! and I can prove it—of bestowing the palest charger upon the least of their pointsmen.

"And no deputy, my poor sir and illustrious Captain, no senator thinks to return the government to some sem-blance of decency; for, if the government closes its eyes to such shady shenanigans, it is because it receives payment in cash for its cooperation.

"(Mr. Papillaud possesses a photograph of Mr. Baudin's last receipt.)

"Ah, what a shame!

"Cordially yours, etc., etc."

This interesting communication was signed by an official from the Ministry of Public Works, who begs Cap not to print his name, because of his little New Year's bonus, which he fears might be affected by this publicity.

CHAPTER XXIX

In which Parmentier's glory is challenged.

Brusquely, Cap turned to the idiotic youth sipping an *iced champagne*[1] beside him.

"Do you read the bulletin of the Academy of Sciences?"

"Never."

"But you must read the pages devoted to the sciences in the daily papers, the informative columns of Émile Gautier, for example?"

"Never."

"I'll wager, then, that you don't reserve the best shelf of your bookcase for that masterpiece of popularization by our friend Georges Claude: *Electricity for Everybody.*"

"What would I do with it?"

"Very well, I won't insist... You are a man like Brunetière, who, not content with declaring Science a failure, further accuses the poor thing of a thousand preposterous sins, notably that of hindering the designs of Providence."

"I don't accuse Science of anything; I'm happy to just ignore it."

"Alas! How many are cut from the same cloth!"

And how we must pity them!

For they miss many unexpected sources of amusement.

For a ready example, I ask that you sample the latest bulletin from our Academy of Sciences.

You will learn, not without legitimate amazement, that the potato is not what our frivolous populace thinks.

The potato is nothing more, if you will excuse the expression, than the fruit of a disease, and a rather shameful disease at that, since it is produced by an ignoble fungus that Noël Bernard, the author of this discovery, does not hesitate to bedeck with the name *fusarium*.

Plant your potatoes in soil devoid of *fusarium*, Noël Bernard asserts, and you will produce no tubers, although the roots of your plants will flourish and fructify to perfection.

Potato roots without potatoes represent, then, the normal state of the plant.

...I don't have the pleasure of Mr. Noël Bernard's acquaintance, but I can see from here the revolting smugness with which he advances his possibly scientific, assuredly monstrous, assertion.

He practically forms a society against the *fusarium*.

But he goes further.

The noble fame of Parmentier, so pure, finds no favor with a creature like this Bernard.

Parmentier, according to our naturalist, never introduced the potato into France.

It was, it appears, a certain Clusius who took care of it before him.

But because Clusius, a conscientious agronomist, was careful to plant his potatoes only in ground free from *fusarium*, no tubers appeared...

Parmentier just didn't check first.

Hence his incontestable notoriety.

But Mr. Noël Bernard was watching.

.....

You're as zealous as a saint, Bernard![2] Too much so. I understand and approve wholeheartedly the battle against tuberculosis, but tubers are another matter.

Besides, the potato, even in its jacket, is big enough to defend itself against your grotesque imputations.

Was it not in reference to the fried potato, so masterful despite its humble appearance, that Victor Hugo once said, "Tuber spelled backwards is rebut"?

Notes:

1. Into a cobbler glass of crushed ice, add a teaspoon of Curaçao, and another of Maraschino, fill with dry Saint-Marceaux, and stir. When ready to serve, add, without stirring, a few drops of a good *crème de vanille.*

2. I didn't do it on purpose.

CHAPTER XXX

Arctic fox within the reach of the smallest budget.

"Another little whiskey cocktail, Cap?"

"Gladly, but just a little one; I'm in a hurry."

"Where are you off to?"

"Today I preside over a meeting of the administrative council of the *General Society of Parisian Furriers*."

On seeing my astonishment, Cap explained in a few words the objectives of this new company. A good prospect for the small investor:

Everybody knows the high prices commanded by skins and furs, unless they come from our own domestic rabbits.

The arctic fox, to cite only one creature, attains prices which prohibit its purchase by, for example, the wives of our humble road workers.

To what can we attribute these discouragingly high prices?

Quite simply to the lands, as distant as they are polar, to which the intrepid hunter must go to track these exorbitant animals, to the thousand difficulties and expenses accompanying the operation, and finally to the high customs fees that importers must pay to bring their precious merchandise under the skies of France.

The "General Society of Parisian Furriers" hopes to remedy this state of affairs, by bringing within the reach of the smallest budget furs now affordable only to our affable princes of finance, their wives, and their daughters.

But, I hear you cry, the "General Society of Parisian Furriers" will lose an insane amount of money in this business.

No, I reply coolly, the "General Society of Parisian Furriers" will reap enormous profits, for, after a rather large initial investment, its daily expenses will be insignificant.

The "General Society of Parisian Furriers" proposes to build in Paris—or, to be precise, under Paris—vast installations in which all of the fur-bearing animals that usually inhabit North America, Canada, Labrador, Alaska, etc., etc., will live and multiply, like rabbits in their warrens.

Thanks to, it must be admitted, a substantial bribe delivered into the hands of Mr. Paul Escudier and several indelicate ediles *ejusdem farinæ,* the "General Society of Parisian Furriers" has obtained the exclusive use, for a period of ninety-nine years, of the Paris catacombs.

To transform these catacombs into an immense icehouse with septentrional temperatures and polar lighting, and to stock the vast cellars with the aforementioned animals, is this not mere child's play?

You get the idea, I think!

And do you not see, you valiant French businessmen, the opportunity for small investors that I mentioned above?

I must stress, however, that there is no time to lose.

.....

P. S. As I expected, my simple outline of the plans for that magnificent enterprise, the "General Society of Parisian Furriers," has provoked understandable emotion in the interesting world of French business.

The idea, in fact, of transforming the catacombs into vast simili-polar refrigerators where one might raise animals with luxuriant fur, could not help but garner a sympathetic response, both encouraging and flattering. From a thousand departments, without exaggeration, have rained subscriptions, advice, requests for information, and applications for employment in the business (anything at all, adds one poor soul).

From this voluminous correspondence I will quote the two following letters, both curious, although for different reasons:

"Dear and glorious Captain,

"Like you, I believe the 'General Society of Parisian Furriers' has a glorious future before it: when you can obtain an arctic fox fur, for example, at a cost not appreciably higher than that of a rabbit skin, you may be sure that such an enterprise could realize profits hitherto unknown to the excellent Mr. Révillon, or to his colleagues in the fur trade.

"Well, my dear sir, I am going to propose a way to increase those profits in appreciable proportions.

"Hear me out, I beg of you.

"In addition to the equipment required by the demands of your operation, what prevents you from developing the 'picturesque' aspect, such as boulders, caverns, brooks, little lakes, trappers' cabins, and even—why not? and what can't we do, thanks to electricity?—the aurora borealis, the midnight sun, and other meteorological phenomena so plentiful in those climes?

"You could then charge admission, and bring in a great number of the curious, who would never tire of such a wonderful spectacle.

"But, you will object, won't these curious, coming from outside and suddenly entering such a cold environment (15 or 20 degrees below zero) risk immediately contracting a fine case of pneumonia, the standard procedure for what we call a 'heat and cold'?

"No, for I have anticipated the problem.

"An ad hoc changing room will furnish our curious with a little outfit similar to those worn by stalwart Canadian hunters.

"But, you continue to object, will our polar bears be

reasonable enough to contemplate all of those gawking tourists with a calm eye and an indolent claw?

"Certainly, for I have again anticipated the problem.

"Over the warm clothing described above, the gawking tourists, as you call them, would wear a suit of armor, like the armor of our valiant knights, but aluminum, to make it lighter.

"You can see that I have anticipated everything.

"In the hope, etc., etc.

"Yours, etc., etc.

"EUGENE."

The other letter, I am afraid, emanated from someone not particularly serious, although rather informal:

"My dear old Captain,

"Pretty neat, that thing of yours about sticking the Septentrion and all those fancy furry critters into the catacombs!

"But aren't you afraid that the opulent beasties will get homesick?

"I see only one solution to the dilemma: distract them by singing, from dawn to dusk, the prettiest tunes from their native villages.

"And, to heighten the illusion, who, if you please, will you get to perform this brilliant repertory?

"Why, of course! Polaire in person, the Polaire star herself!

"Yours,

"VICTOR."

Mr. Victor's harmless joke will not prevent the "Society of Parisian Furriers" from climbing, with a sure hand, the ladder of success.

CHAPTER XXXI

*Street vendors explained by Captain Cap,
and by Mr. Salomon Reinach.*

If we are to believe Captain Cap—and why doubt his word?—he plans to organize, next June 31, a rather unusual convention.

An international convention of street vendors—or, to give them their euphonious French name, "camelots."

Camelots from all over the world will attend this assembly, the first of its kind, but, let us hope, one to be followed by many more.

At the top of its agenda, this charming organization states:

"What is a *camelot*?"

"Nothing."

"What must he become?"

"Everything."

Captain Cap is quite knowledgeable about the history of *camelots*, from the distant past up to the present.

"Waiter!" he cried, "two well-mixed *pick-me-ups!*" [1]

Then, comfortably settled into his tall armchair, he delivered this interesting speech:

Contrary to the idea generally circulated in the uninteresting milieu of shallow minds, the occupation of *camelot*, far from being a recent creation, can be traced back to the earliest days of humanity.

The first *camelot* mentioned in history is the very one who gave his name to the burgeoning industry; and he was not, I hasten to add, a mere nobody! The son of a king, if you please! The son of Lot, king of the Moabites!

Cham Lot—for that was his name—suffered intense sorrow on seeing his mother—whom he adored—transformed, following certain painful incidents which the reader will thank us not to recall, into a pillar of salt.

Wishing to forget such an unpleasant memory (put yourself in his place, if you have any feeling for your mother!), Cham Lot hesitated awhile between intemperance and travel.

Finally, he opted for the latter; but, always a practical boy at heart (young Moabites are still renowned today for their consummate skill in business), Cham Lot took with him several chariots filled with assorted merchandise, obtained at insignificant prices and requiring little room, which he could then retail himself, in different countries, without the assistance of often indelicate servants.

Cham Lot quickly became popular throughout Asia, his bankroll fattened before his eyes, and his grief faded; so much so that, after a while, the brave lad was the first to laugh at the curious accident that had befallen his poor mama.

Cham Lot's example bore fruit: many young men spread throughout the neighboring countries, hawking a thousand different items, which, with strident cries, they identified as to name, use, merits, and price.

In imitation, the people gave to these clamorous individuals the name of their originator: Cham Lot.

The name remained, and has trespassed[2] the ages.

.....

Proud of their quasi-royal origins, our modern *camelots* seek a new awakening in their organization, an awakening leading to greater profits and honors.

Their convention will, no doubt, teem with many interesting details, but it is their tournament that will most fascinate, I think, our capital.

For the congress is to be followed by a tournament.

Thirty seven thousand *camelots* from the four corners of the globe will roam the streets of Paris, competing with one another in the exercise of their lively industry, and trying to sell to alarmed passersby a, no doubt, heteroclite assortment of items.

P. S. Never, I admit, would I have recognized Mr. Salomon Reinach in the gentleman who appeared so politely at the threshold of my studio, top hat in hand.

I was particularly unlikely to recognize him, given

that—let us continue our confession—this was the first time that I ever had occasion to meet him.

Mr. Salomon Reinach has many faults; but nobody, I imagine, would think of contesting his unparalleled authority in all that concerns the knowledge and interpretation of the Bible.

And it was precisely because of that knowledge that Mr. Salomon Reinach, overcoming his natural timidity, decided to seek me out.

Let us turn the floor over to our erudite exegete:

"In your last article,[3] honored sir, an error crept in; one which, if left uncorrected, might well tarnish Captain Cap's solid reputation for scientific precision.

"Cham Lot was, as you say, the first *camelot* mentioned in the Bible; however, he was not Lot's son, as you state, but only his son-in-law.

"Having come from Ethiopia, in Chaldea, Cham—he was then known simply as Cham—was received warmly by Lot's family.

"What had to happen happened: seduced by the charms of Ossa, one of Lot's daughters, Cham easily captured the heart of the beautiful child, and soon, despite the resistance of Mrs. Lot, who disliked negroes—Cham was black—he married her, and added his father-in-law's name to his own."

(Ossa Lot was the prettiest and liveliest of Abraham's nieces. Her features, according to Mr. Salomon Reinach, were strikingly similar to those of our delicious contemporary, Eve Lavillière.)

"Let us quickly pass over the painful incidents that occurred after the marriage, and proceed, without further delay, to the curious adventures in Sodom: 'Flee,' one of the angels told the Lot family, 'but don't even think about looking back, or else...'

"The angel had not finished.

"Sodom burned, with its wicked citizens as combustibles.

"An idea suddenly popped into Cham's diabolical brain.

"'Turn around,' he told his mother-in-law, 'it's a sight worth seeing.'

"Mechanically, Mrs. Lot looked back.

"Oh, it didn't take long!

"In less than a fourth of a second, the good woman was nothing but a heap of sodium chloride.

"Somewhat surprised, but overwhelmed by terror, the Lot family pursued its flight into Canaan, from where our friend Cham returned several weeks later.

"The negro had an idea.

"Between two flat stones, he soon reduced his mother-in-law's remains to powder.

"He divided the salt into a multitude of little packets, which he then sold in the neighboring countries.

"Let me add that the idea of realizing such an unexpected profit from his mother-in-law filled our friend Cham

Lot with joy.

"It is probably to their ancestor's cheerful disposition that today's *camelots* owe their incontestable gaiety."

Notes:

1. The *pick-me-up*, as its name indicates, is recommended as a tonic. To obtain it, put into a silver goblet cracked ice, a tablespoon of lemon juice, another of grenadine, and a third of aged kirsch. Shake, strain, and pour. Fill the glass with Saint-Marceaux and a slice of orange.

2. "Trespass" is here used in the sense of "go across."

3. I had, in fact, published an account of Captain Cap's researches in a major newspaper.

Translator's Notes

XVI: The Pasteur Filter was actually developed by both Charles Chamberland and Louis Pasteur in 1884. Unlike Cap's filter, it made water nicer.

Major Heitner frequently appeared in Allais's stories: Jean Veber even drew a caricature in the *Journal*, showing him drinking with Allais and the Captain. Heitner was a friend of the writer Tristan Bernard, who shepherded a novel of his (*Le Satyre Intermittent*) into publication in 1925. Heiner also appeared as a character actor in movies in the '20s and '30s, particularly those of Tristan's son, Raymond Bernard.

It is an old French folk belief that heat followed by cold invariably makes you ill. It may not be true.

Hannibal did not do well in Capua.

In his 1892 book *Degeneration* (*Entartung*), Max Nordau became quite upset about the art and literature of the time.

XVII: Despite the chapter heading, it is not Cap who makes the ascension.

La Maison Stern is still in business, selling engraved calling cards to discerning clients.

Marcellin Berthelot made many important discoveries

in chemistry, particularly in the synthesis of organic compounds, but probably not in the technique of auto-inflation.

Le Crime du Pecq! ou Fenayrou l'assassin d'Aubert was a murder ballad by Rokada, published in 1882. The murder in question was that of Louis Aubert, killed by Marin Fenayrou, his wife Gabrielle, and his brother Lucien.

Alphonse Allais visited Tadoussac with Paul Fabre in 1894. E. D. and B. de C. are unidentified.

XVIII: As the mention of Tourtel beer intimates, Allais was not above a bit of product placement. Once one of the great breweries, the place where Pasteur studied fermentation, it now produces only a non-alcoholic beverage.

XIX: Marcel Prévost was better known for his novel *Les Demi-Vierges,* which deplored the effects of Parisian life and education on innocent young schoolgirls.

XXI: The Comiot was, in fact, a *"moto-cycle,"* a motorcycle with sidecar.

Gustave Canet's cannon was used in the Sino-Japanese war, where it was discovered to have many technical problems.

XXIII: Léon Mougeot was Under Secretary of State for the Telegraph and Post Office from 1898 to 1902; he was known as a reformer. He also often cut a burlesque figure in Allais's columns. Following a piece on reusing postage stamps, Allais reported that Mougeot bellowed insults at him and tried to butt him in the stomach, and that the quarrel escalated to a duel with pistols in the Hall of Mirrors at Versailles.

Transformism is more usually associated with Lamarck.

XXIV: The Lebel, designed by Nicolas Lebel in 1886, became the standard rifle for the French army.

XXV: The Lexoviani are the people of Lisieux, near Allais's home town, Honfleur.

Paul Deschanel was a politician, later to become president. As far as I know, he was not a particularly picky eater.

Justin Marie Marcellin Lucas-Champonnière was a surgeon, as well as editing the magazine that the Captain so enjoys.

Le Marchand de Merde was offered to the world by Alexis Piron in 1736. In it, Arlequin, to stop Gilles from shitting on doorsteps, convinces him that he's wasting valuable merchandise; Gilles then hawks a barrel of shit around town until it's broken over his head. The play is regarded as either the apex or nadir of a certain genre of theater.

XXVI: Émile Gautier wrote his column, *Chroniques documentaires,* for *Figaro.* He also had quite a career as an anarchist, including a prison term.

XXVII: In order for this to make any sense at all, at all, I had to put a Dutchman with bad English in place of an American with bad French, entailing other ancillary changes. The original eye rhymes, if you're curious, were: *Aigues, cigües, ligues;* and *tient, quotient, balbutient.*

XXVIII: Adolphe Papillaud, a writer for *La Libre Parole,* received the letter from Major Henry that touched off the Dreyfus Affair. Pierre Baudin was the Minister of Public Works.

XXIX: Antonin-Auguste Parmentier promoted potato consumption in the 18th century.

Georges Claude was an active inventor and engineer, known as "the Edison of France"; among other things, he commercialized neon lighting. He later spent World War II collaborating with the Nazis, which did not help his reputation.

Ferdinand Brunetière began his career as a freethinker,

but surprised his readers with an attack on science in an article in 1895 (*Après une visite au Vatican*). It was a turning point; he became an ardent religionist after that.

Noël Bernard wrote a couple of books on the potato. I don't know how his fusarium theory has held up.

Carolus Clusius introduced both the potato and the tulip into Europe in the 16th century. It was Parmentier, though, who convinced people to eat their tubers.

Allais here parodies a tag by Hugo, *"dans connaître, il y a naître"* (In "to know" there is "to be born"), with *"dans tubercule, il y a Hercule"* (In "tuber" there is "Hercules"). Nobody said translation was easy.

XXX: Paul Escudier was the deputy of the 9th arrondissement; he did other things as well.

Louis-Victor Révillon and his company, Révillon Frères, did indeed make money in the fur trade.

Polaire was the professional name of Émile Marie Rouchard, who made herself conspicuous with her radically corseted figure, nose ring, and outrageous behavior both on and off stage.

XXXI: Salomon Reinach was better known as an archeologist. I'm not sure what his faults were. It could be the fact that he wrote a book on Schopenhauer, a philosopher Allais always mocked; it could be a whiff of anti-semitism.

Eve Lavillière was the stage name of Eugenie Fenaglio, who was indeed a famous beauty. She later found religion, and lived as a recluse.

PART FOUR
The Sanatorium of the Future

CHAPTER XXXII

The sanatorium of the future.

On all sides, one hears nothing but talk of "sanatoriums."

.....

My dear typographers, please have the courtesy to open one of your most comfortable parentheses.

(In the plural, if certain gentlemen will excuse me, I do not hesitate to write "sanatoriums"; and my attitude, in this matter, will change only upon that improbable day when, generalizing their pedantry, those certain gentlemen say "aquaria," "harmonia," etc.

Follow my reasoning:

When a foreigner becomes a French citizen, does that not imply that he agrees to embrace our laws?

It is the same for words.

Once an exotic term enters our language, it should submit to our rules without grumbling, however tyrannical or arbitrary they may seem, or else return to its squalid little town and leave us in peace!

When a lady tells me that she has heard some magnificent "soli," I immediately inquire after the health of her "gigoli" (she usually looks like the type!).

If the word is from a dead language, let us urge the poor beggar to hasten back to the peace of its sepulcher, and put an end to the question!)

.....

On all sides, then, one hears nothing but talk of sanatoriums.

And people not only talk about them, which would never suffice to vanquish tuberculosis; they construct and inaugurate them.

Not in sufficient numbers, alas!, but everything must have a beginning, no?

I will not presume to give you a lesson on the proper conditions for the management of a sanatorium.

You know that an establishment of this kind must realize all that the world has to offer concerning isolation, fresh air, and temperature.

Furthermore, they do not swarm in myriads, the places suited for such an enterprise.

And then, there are the neighbors, who scream like a fresh hog[1] and complain of contamination whenever anyone suggests installing, next to their properties, mansions, or hovels, one of these celebrated sanatoriums.

Any sentient being, then, can only shudder at the relentlessly mounting ravages of this terrible scourge, and the few barricades which, despite our science and all of our fear, we manage to erect against it, pathetically.

Sad! Sad! Sad!

He who discovers the secret of cheap and plentiful sanatoriums will have rendered—in advance, we doff our hat to him—one of those services to humanity that make a man the equal of Jenner, Lister, or Pasteur!

We need not await this man.

He is here already, for he is none other than our glorious Captain Cap.

A spacious and ideal location, fresh air, constant warm weather, no neighbors, no rent: what more do you want for a sanatorium truly worthy of the name?

"Where is it, that I may run to it?" you smile, incredulous.

...I will not keep you in suspense.

The location that Cap has discovered for all future sanatoriums is the Gulf Stream.

I will not belabor the point; you understand.

Did I exaggerate by extolling the incomparable advantages of this gigantic spa, this—the term is fitting—hot springs?

It goes without saying that the design for our new sanatorium will more closely resemble in its general outline the ship that sails the seas than the terrestrial abode.

Without even mentioning that the poor feverish, as Michel Corday calls them, will be able to amuse themselves by fishing, and, to a great extent, to live upon their catch, so rich in phosphorous: a diet recommended, in this case, by our finest practitioners.

It is all quite simple, as you can see; but you still have to think of it.

Notes:

1. Some people say "scream like a foxhound." The true expression is "scream like a fish-hawk." But, apart from the fact that the fish-hawk is a bird barely familiar even to Louis Ternier, the impeccable ornithologist, I prefer "fresh hog," this animal recommending itself to us by its uniquely discordant squeal, particularly during the period immediately preceding its introduction to the joyous butcher, master of our destinies.

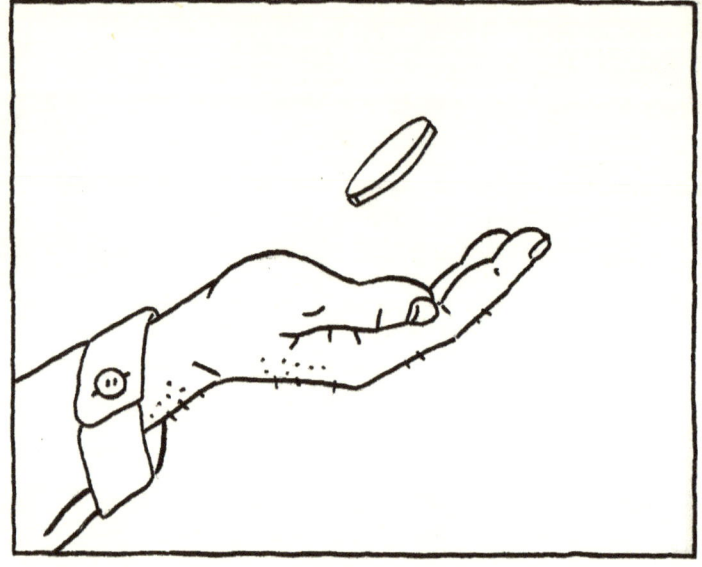

CHAPTER XXXIII

A new aspect of metallotherapy.

Back in the era—and it doesn't make us any younger—when I haunted the Latin Quarter, the medical students that I used to have the custom of living with[1] eagerly discussed a new method for alleviating the suffering of humanity, which had been simultaneously invented by two erudite clinicians, Dr. Burq and Dr. Dumontpallier: metallotherapy, whose name alone makes further description superfluous.

Around the same time, there was also great interest, in the same neighborhood, in the curious research of Dr. Luys, who, in la Salpêtrière (I believe), simply held certain drugs to his patients' feet, to, among other things, cure them of intercostal neuralgia, a simple head cold, ringworm, etc., etc.[2]

You must admit that it all seems quite marvelous, as Mr. Gaston Méry, our active municipal councillor, would say.

I don't know what happened, since then, to Burq and Dumontpallier's system of metallotherapy, but I recall that the supposed "action of medication at a distance" soon earned Dr. Luys's reputation more than one incredulous and mocking smirk.

Well, those who smirked were wrong to smirk, and the little incident that he who writes these lines witnessed this very morning, to his amazement, reunites in common joy the shades³ of Luys, Burq, and Dumontpallier.

I found myself, then, around half past eleven—as if by chance—on the terrace of the Paix cafe, in the company of Captain Cap.

That perfect gentleman told me the following story:

"You see in me a man charged with a pleasant mission. Having lost the sum of five francs in a bet that I had contracted with Madame X. Y. Z.,⁴ I saw my losing stake returned: "Keep your dollar," the lovely winner insisted, "and give it on my part to the first truly interesting beggar that you meet."

Cap was at that point in his story, when suddenly there appeared at our table that poor indigent so familiar to all Parisians who frequent the area from the Madeleine Church to the Opera House.

I refer to that sorry figure with the dull red hair, whose walk, whose implacable walk, is nothing but a never-ending succession of jolts throughout his entire body.

"Well," cried Cap, "there's my beggar!"

Extracting the five franc coin from his pocket, my friend pressed it into the agitated palm of the twitching hand.

Suddenly—I could not believe my eyes—all shaking stopped in our man's head, in his arms, and in his legs!

The five franc coin before him, he at once became as immobile as a statue of bronze.

This extremely curious cure, sadly, lasted no more than a minute, at the end of which our unfortunate resumed his usual agitation.

Keenly interested in such an unexpected reaction, and firmly resolved to pursue its development, we followed the trail, Cap and I, of our new subject.

Soon, he stopped under a gateway, drew from his pocket the five franc coin, and thoroughly studied both sides (that is, both heads and tails); he then entered a saloon where he absorbed, in less time than it takes to write it, one of those absinthes in which the spoon stands easily upright.

During all this time, he never trembled once.

.....

Without jumping hastily to conclusions, may we be permitted, from now on, to presume that silver is a metal that need not be ingested, as was formerly believed, to have a marked sedative effect on nervous disorders?

Notes:

1. I beg my gracious readers to excuse this preposterous way of expressing myself: I have, at the moment, in my house, a Belgian family, who are quite decent people, but whose language has somewhat bled into mine.

2. Same observation as above.

3. If among these gentlemen, one is not yet deceased, I respectfully ask him not to be cross with me. A bit of patience, and it will come.

4. These initials barely veil the identity of an extremely charming young woman in the foreign colony: Madame Xavière Yturbide-Zevaco.

CHAPTER XXXIV

Let us cross rivers on bridges of crocodiles.

L etters such as the following honor the citizens who write them as much as the man to whom they are addressed.

Therefore I do not hesitate to publish this letter, even before reading it:

"Dear sir and honorable Captain!

"Before I begin, permit me to doff my kepi before the ardent patriot whose ever wakeful spirit has never lost sight of our national well-being, even to the point of assuring it with the help of the most unexpected animals.

"Your idea of training anti-cyclist military dogs, as well as equally military anti-canine fleas, is among those that have made you the envy of Europe.

"Furthermore, your invention of bullets loaded with itching powder clearly shows your great humanitarianism, allied with implacable nationalism.

"And more recently, did not your falcons trained to burst enemy balloons attract the attention of a great neighboring nation, which my position in the army prevents me from naming more clearly?

"I have not mentioned your ingenious torpedo-bearing crocodiles, because that is precisely the subject that has led me to contact you today.

"Yes, Captain, you are perfectly correct when you affirm that the crocodile is the most trainable of animals.

"Many of my comrades, officers in the Sudan, have told me that, raised from the egg and treated with kindness, the crocodile becomes attached to man, and strives to perform the thousand little services that its natural disposition permits.

"It would thus be an error, as you have so well demonstrated, not to profit from such favorable dispositions.

"...Since my last maneuvers, I have been principally engaged in studying new methods for crossing rivers, when there is neither bridge nor ford at hand.

"You may smile, perhaps, but the method that seemed to work the best was rafts improvised from empty canteens, wrapped with straw in waterproof sacks.

"Often during our experiments, my comrades and I, we thought of you, and mourned the absence of your resourceful imagination.

"And now, without your even knowing, you have set us on the right path with your stories about crocodiles!

"To some extent proverbial, the insubmersibility of this saurian proves that old Archimedes fell short of the truth when, stark naked, in the street, he proclaimed his famous principle, to the great joy of the urchins of Syracuse, who chanted in unison "Eureka! Eureka!" like a playground taunt.

"The crocodile bridge!

"Yes, that's the crux of the matter.

"Therefore, may the gentlemen of the artillery, whose concern this is, hesitate no longer! May a special detail of crocodile-pontonier trainers be organized without delay!

"Who knows? This may be our salvation.

"Please accept, etc.

"GUY DE POAST,
"First lieutenant, infantry.

Of course, our honorable correspondent's idea is a seductive one, but, as Cap says, you will once again see bureaucratic inertia at work.

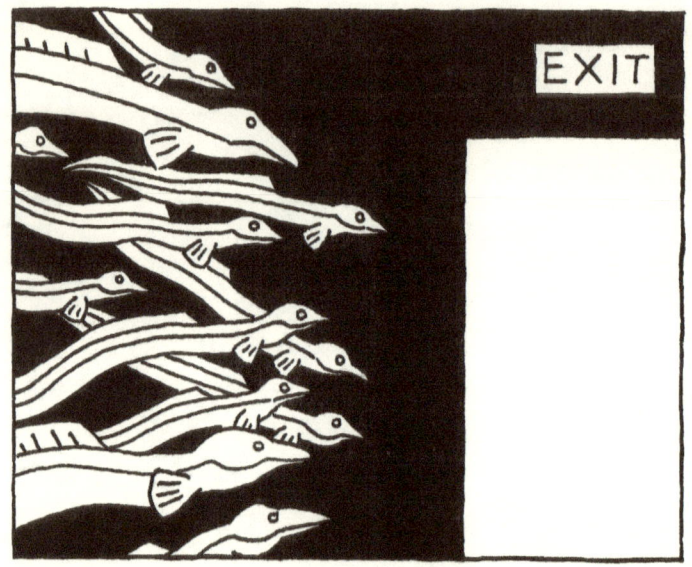

CHAPTER XXXV

Safety in theaters.

The safety of theatergoers is one of those problems that should leave no thinker indifferent, even though no recent catastrophe has made this gloomy subject a topical one.

Every evening, an innumerable crowd of foreigners packs our places of amusement: French hospitality demands that we roast as few of them as possible.

What constitutes the real danger in these accidents is not so much the fire itself, as the unbelievable panic that manifests itself at the start of the incident, and causes stampede, blocking, trampling.

A crowd which, terrified, surges into the aisles of a theater is a cork that swells in the narrow neck of a bottle.

.....

All naturalists will tell you that among eels, accidental death by the combustion of a theater, or some other pleasure spot in flames, is among the rarest of occurrences.

To what may we attribute this apparently curious immunity?

To this, quite simply: that the eel, gifted by nature with a perfectly smooth body, as if lubricated, can, at the first alarm, slide and slither, and promptly reach the outside, without any epidermal roughness to hinder its sinuous progress.

The experiment is an easy one: fill a theater with eels, suddenly shout some cry of alarm, such as "Here come the Tartars!", and you will marvel at the speed with which the supple little audience will evacuate the building.

.....

Cannot humanity draw some profitable lesson from this example?

In good faith, Captain Cap thought for a moment that there was, and he proposed to the appropriate authorities a plan for a sort of garment to be worn by the spectators, in the form of a duster, with, instead of cloth, peach skin, simple peach skin.

Having, after many long hours of research, discovered that the skin of a dead eel does not possess the same slippery qualities as that of a living one, he decided to replace it with peach skin, whose properties, in that respect, are known and appreciated by connoisseurs.

The plan, of course, having met only snickering disdain from the big cheeses, his philanthropic work went no further.

A new system towards the same end seems to him more practical.

Could we not, he insinuates, compel theater directors to transform the aisles of their establishments into moving aisles, similar to the rolling sidewalk, you remember, at the 1900 Exposition,[1] in the Champ de Mars?

The same for the stairs, which would be replaced by moving ramps, like those seen in our Exposition, with, however, the difference that they would be, if you will excuse the expression, "descensional."

In case of fire, a simple switch sets the machinery in action.

And so, no more stampede, or, if stampede, no more catastrophe, because everyone would land in the street, automatically.

Notes:

1. How long ago it was!

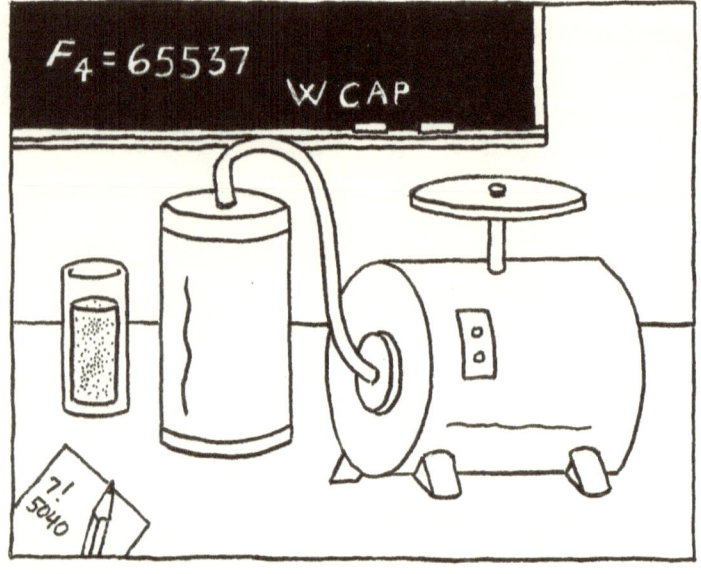

CHAPTER XXXVI

*In which Russia tries to steal a bit of
Captain Cap's thunder.*

I leave you to imagine the sparkle in my eyes when,
scanning the contents of the very interesting *Review
of Industrial Chemistry*, I fell upon this title, so full of
interest: "Production of Motive Energy by Microbes. "

At once, I was reminded of an old plan Captain Cap
once devised to activate powerful machines with rotifers,
those ridiculous little creatures that spend their lives turning, turning, without pause, without reason, without purpose, without result, and, as Verlaine would have added,
without hope of hay.

But the *Review of Industrial Chemistry* is too serious a
publication to harbor such tomfoolery.

What then could it be?

Calm yourself; here it is:

"The engineer N. P. Melnikoff, of Odessa"—I copy
verbatim—"has built a miniature model of a machine that
runs on the products of bacterial life.

"The machine still has no real practical application,
having just been born; but it is of great interest, from a
mechanical point of view, for studying bacterial life, and
the energy of its development.

"Mr. N. P. Melnikoff first used the bacterium *Saccharo-
myces cerevisiae,* which produces alcoholic fermentation by
separating the sugar into alcohol and carbonic acid.

"You take a copper container, and introduce glucose, yeast, water, etc.

"The next day, at a temperature of 20 degrees, the container is filled with carbonic acid at a pressure of four and a half atmospheres, corresponding to 15 English pounds of pressure per square inch."

(Why does this Russian inventor use English measures? Is the Alliance then an empty word?)

So, you then need only—I abridge—put your compressed gas to work, which is the beginning of the art.

Pierre Gifford published a book (and neglected to send me a copy) called *The End of the Horse*.

The time is perhaps not so far off when we will write (and not without reason) *The End of Gasoline*, *The End of Electricity*, etc., etc.

With bacteria machines, the future need look no further, for there is no danger of this fuel running short; when there is no more, there is still more!

And then, the great advantage of the Melnikoff system consists above all in the practical use of the residue: about a liter of cognac (?) for every five kilos of glucose.

Good, then! Something tasty!

.....

And now, lest us brutally wrest from Mr. N. P. Melnikoff, of Odessa, the apotheotic crown that he usurps!

Mr. N. P. Melnikoff comes in a distant second in this interesting question.

The first is none other, once again, you guessed it, than our glorious friend Captain Cap.

In fact, some two years ago (I lack the leisure now to check the precise date), upon the Captain's advice, I foresaw a method of reducing the cost of transporting our national wines from their place of harvest to that of consumption.

It was simply a question of transporting them during their fermentation, by using pressurized carbonic acid to move the wheels of the trucks ad hoc.

Let us add, not without some humiliation, that no engineer brought this beautiful dream to reality.

But Russia was there, wide awake!

Long live Russia! Hurray!

CHAPTER XXXVII

In which Captain Cap brings a seductive gleam into the eyes of writers and publishers.

Although absurdly exaggerated by certain crybabies, still astonished that their latest dollop of trash did not sell a hundred thousand copies and one copy, as Dr. Mardrus says, the poor market for books is a painful, but incontestable, phenomenon.

Captain Cap, whom I always consult in such circumstances, gave me an explanation for the problem that reveals, in this eminent economist, as much profound science as solid common sense:

"A book sells well only if many customers present themselves to make its acquisition.

"When there is a mediocre number of clients, the sale of the book will suffer; and the traffic becomes even weaker as the quantity of purchasers diminishes."

"Perfectly reasoned, but the remedy?"

"Oh, the remedy is quite simple! Grant me a bit of your attention."

"I'm all ears."

That the solution offered by the Captain soon be put into practice, we fervently hope, but without premature celebration:

Given equal success, a play performed in a theater earns infinitely more money than a novel sold in a bookstore.

Why?

Because, if you like a play, and want to see it again, you must buy a new ticket every time; whereas, once you have paid for a book, you can read it as often as you please.

Even worse: you can loan the book to thousands of people, without this pullulation of readers depositing one additional denier into the poor author's coffer.

A play you cannot lend to even your most intimate friend.

Describe it? Of course, but that's not the same thing.

Do you grasp the pecuniary difference between the two forms of art?

With the theater (excepting complimentary tickets), there are as many suckers as there are spectators!

With a book... I would prefer not to do the calculation, it would be too depressing!

What is needed, then, is a plan to remedy, vis-à-vis literature, this distressing state of inferiority.

I believe I have found one.

Experience, however, will soon speak more loudly than the cleverest theory.

Learn this, then:

A few books will soon make their appearance, printed in "volatile ink."

Volatile ink is an ink which, exposed to the air, volatilizes—as the name indicates—without leaving the slightest trace.

So that—and you can see the advantages, for both publishers and authors—the same volume, usable by a limited number of readers, must be renewed as soon as its pages have become as white as ermine, that is to say, in short order.

Whether this ingenious stratagem will remedy the unhappy plight of the literati, only the immediate future can tell.

CHAPTER XXXVIII

*In which Captain Cap does not fool
around when he is taken advantage of.*

Having slipped his ten centimes into the slot of the mechanical apparatus, Captain Cap flew into a frightful rage when he saw that nothing budged, and that the promised chocolate bar was not forthcoming.

"Band of thieves!" he fumed.

And he added:

"I will come tonight with a stick of dynamite, and blow up their damn machine."

"That, Captain," I said, "is excessive revenge for a pitiful two sous."

"It's not the two sous! I don't care about the two sous! But I don't like to be taken advantage of."

I know, in fact, few people as susceptible as Cap, at certain times.

All too ready to imagine that the entire human race has bonded together to swindle him, he remains angry, and broods obsessively on brilliant and cruel methods of revenge.

Having noticed one day that his grocer had sold him a 485 gram pound of sugar, he returned the next day, and tossed into the olives and prunes a heaping handful of strychnine.

"It's not the 15 grams of sugar," he explained quietly. "I

don't care about the 15 grams of sugar! But I don't like to be taken advantage of!"

On another occasion, he went even further.

In a hotel in Marseilles where he often stayed, he noticed, as he packed his bags to leave, that he was missing a celluloid collar.

No doubt about it! In his absence, a bellhop had opened the trunk and stolen the item.

Cap did not waste a minute. Instead of returning to Paris, where business called, he boarded a ship for Trieste.

Trieste—who doesn't know this?—is, next to Hamburg, the major European marketplace for wild animals.

The man had the good fortune to find, at once, a true bargain: a mangy adult jaguar, whose unpleasant personality would have tried the patience of a saint, and which he acquired for a ridiculous pittance.

The jaguar was coaxed into a strong trunk, one of those strong trunks in which steel plays a greater part than wicker or waxed canvas.

A swift steamer carried the disgruntled Captain and his ferocious companion back to Marseilles.

...

The jaguar, which, in its natural state, is not noted for unflappable mansuetude, loses even more sociability during a week's sojourn in a trunk, even when its master has taken the precaution of including a dozen kilograms of the very best horse meat.

Our jaguar behaved no differently than the majority of its congeners.

As it happened, the bellhop unwisely decided to appropriate a pocket handkerchief belonging to our friend.

And then, oh, and then! The trunk opened more brusquely than the indiscreet employee had anticipated.

The poor jaguar, happy to finally stretch its cramped

muscles, manifested its joy with a bit of carnage, which included the guilty bellhop, two maids, three tourists, the manager of the hotel, his wife, and a number of other insignificant gentlemen.

When a jaguar is enjoying itself, nothing can stop it.

"Well, sir," Captain Cap concluded cheerfully, "I often returned to that hotel, and never again missed as much as a sleeve button. What can I say? Me, I don't like to be taken advantage of."

CHAPTER XXXIX

Economy linked to well-being.

"Show up," a friendly engineer advised us simply, "at ten twenty-five at the Batignolles station, and you will witness something quite curious indeed."

As you may imagine, we took pains, the Captain and I, not to miss such an opportunity.

At the specified time, we were there.

A train was firing up, ready to leave.

Quite a few well-dressed characters were already there, several of whom sported, in the buttonhole, the red rosette of the Legion of Honor.

"All aboard, please, gentlemen!" cried the friendly engineer mentioned above.

I forgot to add, but I think there is still time to correct this negligence, that it was an uncomfortably hot day.

We boarded the train.

A whistle rent the air, and the train started.

The train was one of those trains that resemble all other trains.

It was composed of a number of cars, which were themselves subdivided into a certain number of compartments.

So far, then, nothing unusual, nothing new.

I had reached that point in my reflections, when, to my great surprise, I saw all of my traveling companions begin to remove their footwear.

As if it were the most natural thing in the world, they slipped off their boots and their stockings.

They then rolled their trousers and undergarments up to the knee.

After which, one of them lifted a metal plate in the floor, and revealed a large basin filled with water, a basin that took up the entire compartment.

And the passengers all settled into the comfort of a foot bath.

My word, we did as they.

You cannot imagine, if you have not tried it yourself, the exquisite sensation of a foot bath on a train: it is delicious.

I understood then the experiment that I was witnessing.

Besides, a decorated gentleman filled me in, with a graciousness that one seldom encounters nowadays in high administrative circles.

The installation of foot baths in railway cars will produce several excellent results.

For travelers, comfort, health, cleanliness.

For the railway, an enormous saving on fuel.

Judge for yourself.

When poured into the aforesaid basins, the water is at a temperature of approximately 15 degrees.

Contact with the passengers' feet heats it rather quickly (especially in summer) to the temperature of the human foot, 37 degrees.

At that point, the tepid water is poured into the boiler, and replaced by cooler water.

That makes twenty-two degrees of heat that cost nothing to the administration!

I have mislaid the paper on which I took my notes, but I seem to recall that human heat, captured and used in this way, represents a saving of 100 grams of coal per passenger and per kilometer.

This, I believe, is unique in the annals of the great railways: a reform that unites in common satisfaction both the shareholders and the public.

"This," concluded Cap, "is successful collectivism, that's what this is."

And we celebrated the occasion, with, since it was such a hot day, a copious *champagne julep*.[1]

Notes:

1. Into a large glass, place three or four sprigs of fresh mint, a teaspoon of sugar, and a jigger of cognac. Fill with crushed ice, a jigger of yellow Chartreuse, top off with dry Saint-Marceaux, and stir well. Soak a sprig of mint in lemon and put it in the center of the glass; add seasonal fruits, drizzle with a good rum, and sprinkle with sugar. Drink through a straw.

CHAPTER XL

*In which we see the evolution of both
kangaroos and Mr. Brunetière.*

T he many people who, taking advantage of the
recent fine weather, took a stroll in the Bois,
received a bit of a surprise.

A whole family appeared: father, mother, two older
girls, and a little boy, all energetically pedaling away on
tandems painted in Nile green.

There were five tandems for these five persons, and the
second individual on each tandem was none other than a
kangaroo.

Do not gape like that, good people; you read aright: the
second individual on each tandem was indeed a kangaroo.

And the entire group, animals, people, machines, sailed
by like a dream.

I happened to be in the area myself, taking a spin on the
three-seater that I had just purchased with Brunetière and
Captain Cap.

Not without some difficulty, we followed the strange
velocade[1] to Suresnes.

There, before a humble pub, the entire family dismounted.

The kangaroos alone remained seated, each stabilizing
the vehicle with its powerful tail against the ground.

And there could be no more comical sight than those

animals, solemn and obedient, awaiting their masters in perfect stillness, like English flunkeys behind their lords' carriages.

Soon, before an excellent *American lemonade,*[2] we made the acquaintance of the whole family.

With his usual joviality, Brunetière introduced us, Cap and me, in the most flattering terms he could find.

In her turn, the youngest of the girls introduced herself, then presented her family: her papa, her mama, her sister, and her little brother.

Australians.

These ladies and gentlemen had a good laugh at our astonishment, and informed us that, in their country, the *kangacycle* is as common as the simple bicycle is in ours.

The kangaroo, an intelligent, docile, and vigorous animal, provides Australians nowadays all of the services that Eskimos demand of their reindeer. More, in fact, since the Eskimo cannot hold a candle to the Australian in the matter of industry.

The kangaroo—and anyone who remembers the boxing kangaroos at the New Circus and the Folies-Bergère will not disagree—the kangaroo is gifted with supple and robust forequarters (without prejudice, besides, to the uncommon strength of its posterior members).

Ignoring the vague sentimentaleries that make our old Europe so ludicrous, Australians have long utilized the many qualities of the kangaroo.

One of their latest applications was precisely the *kangacycle* that I just mentioned.

Comfortably installed on a little platform behind the second wheel, the kangaroo uses its forepaws to operate a pedal which could, if required, suffice to operate the vehicle.

I will not insist on the invaluable assistance given so

tangibly (I could even say *tandemly*) by the vigorous creature, but I will emphasize the advantages of the perfect stability, both in motion and repose, afforded by the kangaroo's long and solid tail.

No more falls, no more skids, no more need to dismount at every stop.

What is more, the kangaroo can provide the valuable service of guarding the machine in your absence, as would the most faithful dog.

Brunetière marveled openly at such ingenuity.

Cap said nothing, but, all the same, I could tell that the *kangacycle* had taken the wind out of his sails.

Notes:

1. We say *cavalcade*.

2. *American lemonade* is made like ordinary lemonade, with sugar, lemon juice, and seltzer. The only difference is that you add a bit of port.

CHAPTER XLI

An excerpt from a talk by Captain Cap on lighthouses.

The frightful catastrophe of the *Drummond Castle* brings up again the extremely important question of lighthouses.

Despite the claims of certain English papers, the coasts of France are as well illuminated as those of England, equipped with relatively the same number of lighthouses, with lights fully as intense as those on the other side of the Channel.

Sadly, though, there are cases where lighthouses, as numerous and dazzling as they may be, are not enough to warn the poor navigator of danger.

Fog is sometimes so thick at sea that the poor sailor cannot see the light of his pipe.

Our sense of sight being absolutely useless, in this case, we thought to call upon our sense of hearing; and so we invented the foghorn, with its lugubrious and cautionary bellow.

But this device did not yield the expected results, for, however powerful a foghorn may be, its range has strict limits.

Another inconvenience of the foghorn: even the most experienced sailor can easily mistake the direction of the sound. At a certain distance, his reckoning may be off by as much as 90 degrees.

What then?

Allow me to relate a personal fact:

Several years ago, I had the opportunity, in I forget which gazette, to discuss this interesting question of lighthouses.

Both sight and hearing, I said, are in many cases not up to the task.

On the other hand, neither the sense of touch nor taste would be, as far as reefs are concerned, of any help.

We are left with the sense of smell.

Nobody, until now, has dreamed of using his nose to sniff out neighboring rocks.

...And so I proposed that a competent committee create odorous buoys for treacherous waters.

Why not?

Picture the scene: a black night made darker by a dense fog. Not a light on land, not a star in the sky!

For music, the whistling of the wind in the rigging, the crashing of waves, the cries of women and children.

Where are they, these poor sailors? God only knows, and even He may not be sure!

Suddenly, the captain gets a whiff of the powerful odor of aged roquefort from NNW, and from SE, a faint aroma of *martini cocktail*.[1]

He consults his map (a map that will be drawn ad hoc), and recognizes his position.

Saved! Thank the Lord!

He steers accordingly, and, an hour later, the ship is docked, and everyone, sailors and passengers, breaks into either hymns of praise, or a good hot grog.

Unfortunately, this is all but a dream.

Routine, damned routine, is in charge, a barrier to all new ideas, all progress, all salvation!

Believe me if you will, but the administration for light-houses did not even acknowledge receipt of my plans for the *smell-buoy*.

Notes:

1. One of the best cocktails when well prepared. Cracked ice, a half tablespoon each of orange bitters, Curaçao, and *crème de noyaux*. Finish with equal parts of gin and Turin vermouth. Shake, strain, and add lemon zest.

CHAPTER XLII

In which, to please the citizens of Paris, it is a question of lowering the price of gas.

"Parisians," cried Cap, "must be stupid indeed to pay six sous for a cubic meter of gas, when they could procure an excellent quality in London for less than a penny."

"Excuse me, Cap, but the transport?"

"The transport, the transport, I was waiting for that! When you say *transport*, you've said it all. Well, my dear friend, not only will the transport cost nothing, it will even be profitable."

You open your eyes at that, dear readers, and your ears even more.

And yet nothing is more true: not only will the transport cost nothing, it will even BE PROF-IT-A-BLE!

Such an assertion requires a smidgen of gloss.

"My dear Captain, you have the floor."

The railways, as well as shipping lines and other companies, charge for the transport of merchandise according to the weight of the commodities.

Now I ask you, what does gas weigh?

Not satisfied with weighing nothing, it pushes its coquetry to the point of weighing less than nothing, due to Archimedes's principle.

(A brief parenthesis, if you will, the time to sip an *Alabazam cocktail*[1]: have you noticed that people always talk about Archimedes's principle, and never about his principles, of which he was, besides, so bereft that he left his bath, and strolled stark naked down the busiest streets of Syracuse, to dry himself, he claimed?)

Logically, then, shipping companies should pay, rather than charge, money for transporting this merchandise of negative weight.

Is that what would happen in practice? I don't think so.

The companies would introduce the question, not negligible, I admit, of volume, and use it to justify enormous fees.

It is here that I offer the resource of the aerostat.

And there, once again, you can lug your stuff around for free, or almost.

And nothing prevents us, my dear friends, from using the nacelle of the balloon to repatriate laundry sent to London by foolish but profitable snobs.

If fifty or sixty thousand Parisian tradesmen were to put my idea into practice, we would see the all-powerful Gas Company lower its prices.

Yes, but there you have it: in France, everyone is happy to complain, but when the time comes to bell the cat, they vanish!

Poor France!

Notes:

1. Crushed ice, a few drops of angostura and lemon, a teaspoon of Curaçao. Fill with cognac, strain, add lemon zest, and serve. This is the *Alabazam*.

CHAPTER XLIII

In which it is a question of the pig, that useful auxiliary to the butcher, as Buffon put it.

And, on this occasion, let me remind you of an anecdote that an old uncle of mine liked to tell, in those bygone days when, a fresh and pink baby, I framed my brow with glossy brown curls.

Two individuals once decided to buy a pig together.

So far, so good.

Conscientiously, they fattened their pig, bringing it a thousand household scraps, bran, and even potatoes.

Throughout this period of overfeeding, perfect harmony never ceased to reign between the two honest co-proprietors.

Here is where things faltered.

One fine day, one of the gentlemen calculated that the pig was ready, and that the hour had sounded to butcher the creature.

Such was not the opinion of the other.

They decided to wait.

A few days passed, and the first owner returned to his plan.

"It's time to kill our pig."

"Not yet! I know what I'm doing: the animal is still not at its best. A bit more time."

The impatient man scratched his head, and, with the air

of one who has made a great decision, announced:

"Listen, old man, do what you like with your half of the pig, but I'm killing mine."

And so he did.

I need not add that by killing his part of the creature, he caused the other portion to pass away as well.

...I remembered this story as I read a stupefying circular that Captain Cap had pressed upon me, with a recommendation to invest.

It concerned a business—a miraculous enterprise, according to the prospectus—devoted to *delarding living pigs*.

The beginning of the brochure, given here verbatim, will enlighten you on the question:

"PORCARINE
"The origin and principle of the invention.

"Even the simplest farmer knows that when a pig has arrived at the proper psychological moment (sic), that is, perfectly fattened, it will allow important portions of its flesh to be eaten by rats.

"The celebrated inventor *M. L. Tourillon,* who sold us his patents, and who remains attached to our society, was struck by this fact, and so conceived his famous *delarding* machine.

"An elastic pantograph and helicoidal razor scoops form the basis, etc., etc."

...This is followed by a detailed description of its operation, and the designation of the future victims, which will belong to the breeds *Middlesex, New Leicester,* and *Tonkinoise.* (The *Craonnaise* breed, apparently, is too fleshy for this type of enterprise. Fortunate breed!)

"...Properly exploited, each pig will *offer* (!!!) 100 kilos of lard a year, that is, a minimum of two hundred francs."

"And the Society for the Protection of Animals, Cap, what will they say?"

"The problem has been anticipated, and a charming little postscript answers all objections in advance: 'To soothe the alarm of the tender-hearted, and to satisfy the Society for the Protection of Animals, the pigs will be anesthetized before undergoing the operation.'"

"We can expect a rise in the sale of chloroform," the Captain concluded.

CHAPTER XLIV

*In which Cap shows by example that he
likes to see for himself.*

"Yes, my friend, I like to see for myself."

"You're a wise man, Captain."

"And so, I've heard it said that on a foggy morning, like this one, a glass of rum is eminently salutary. Let's find out."

A little cafe, just then, beckoned to us:

"Waiter, two glasses of rum."

"Here, gentlemen."

When we had tasted:

"Your rum, waiter, is not so great."

"We have a better one, sir, at sixty centimes the glass."

"I bet it's the same."

"What do you take us for?" the waiter bristled.

"Well, give us two glasses of your better rum. I like to see for myself."

The second rum resembled the first as a brother does his twin.

We left, not without having expressed our discontentment with several vulgar and insulting remarks.

Nearby, a placard set upon a basket of oysters, before a humble wine seller, drew our attention: *Delivered fresh every morning.*

"What a joke!" my friend scoffed. "Delivered fresh!

Fresh from the grocery store, probably. Shall we see for ourselves?"

Nothing whets the appetite like two glasses of bad rum in quick succession: I consented.

We washed down the oysters with a rather brisk white wine, followed by a little rosé from Ardennes whose authenticity my suspicious friend wanted to verify.

The little rosé from Ardennes lent itself so well to sampling that, five minutes later, a bottle of Sauternes replaced it on the table.

"Sauternes! Ah, his Sauternes must be nice!... Well, we'll soon find out."

This system of investigation continued throughout the morning.

Almost all known aperitifs were the object of serious personal inquiry.

"I'll bet you it's not a real Pernod!... I'm sure that quinine isn't really Dubonnet!"

And I, to indulge Cap's obsession, informed myself if the Curaçao was a true Curaçao from Reichoffen, and if the bottle of anisette indeed bore Béranger's signature.

The clock struck twelve.

We were ready to take our leave, when the Captain noticed two men riding by on their tandem, like two kites launched by a master hand.

"Gentlemen, gentlemen! Stop!" cried my friend.

One of the men turned, interrogative.

"Yes, you!" Cap insisted. "Stop right now, both of you!"

The men stopped, dismounted, and approached us.

"Thank you, gentlemen, for complying so graciously to my request. Now that I see that there are two of you, you may continue your promenade."

"But, sir, what is the meaning of this?"

"Oh, my God, it's quite simple! I wanted to assure myself that there are indeed two of you, because, if you were only one, that would mean that I was abominably drunk. I like to see for myself."

And Cap concluded:

"Since we are not drunk, what prevents us from enjoying an excellent *brandy shanteralla?*"[1]

"Nothing, Cap; nothing in the world could prevent such a decision."

Notes:

1. The *brandy shanteralla,* not recommended for the weaker sex, is prepared like this: into cracked ice, pour one tablespoon each of Curaçao, yellow Chartreuse, and anisette; top off with a good cognac.

CHAPTER XLV

The superiority of practice over theory.

I n every trade—proclaimed Captain Cap—in every profession, in every art, one needs experience.

Those who would express a contrary opinion, you must consider sorry imbeciles, or at least dangerous scalawags.

The wisdom of the world—which is by no means foolish—has long said: practice makes perfect, not consulting manuals on basket-weaving or taking political economy courses from our genial comrade Paul Leroy-Beaulieu.

The government has understood this principle so well that it does not hesitate, for example, to build expensive hospitals where it maintains, at considerable expense, a bunch of poor buggers, whom it has previously infected with a thousand different ailments, from simple ecchymosis to imminent maternity.

All to complete the theoretical education of our future medics, and to train them in practices on which the health and existence of us distinguished tradespeople depends.

Inspired by these hospitals, there was once talk of creating in Paris, and in some of the larger towns in the provinces, courtrooms for the poor, where young lawyers and judges could practice on trials for insignificant citizens, cases whose outcome would not affect the greater social order, and where a future mouthpiece might, without serious repercussions, learn his tricks.

The project was shelved for lack of funds.

...But let us return to medicine.

Although many civilian doctors find ample opportunity for application in their hospitals, military doctors are often deprived of the material for serious practice.

Broken legs are common, but a chest shattered by a melinite shell is rarely encountered, nowadays.

Typhoid blossoms everywhere, but a good slash across the face with a sword is a rarity.

And Lebel bullets that pierce the body? How many of you can boast to have seen them?

We can call upon the accidents in our hexagonal nation, and on a few episodes from our colonial expansion.

It is not enough!

From this sorry state of affairs results a painful veneer of amateurism, which has spread over all of our military doctors for the last thirty years.

Many of these practitioners have never seen, seen with their own eyes, the slightest trace of a wound from a firearm.

And so, when the Great Day arrives, will we be able to trust them?

Will they know how to dress our glorious, but perhaps mortal, injuries?

Prey to these legitimate preoccupations, I, Captain Cap, beseech two great European nations—the time has not yet come to name them—to form a particularly interesting pact.

These two nations, enemies for a good third of a century, will agree, next summer, to conduct important joint maneuvers.

An army of the first will march upon an army of the second.

The rifles and cannons will be loaded with real ammunition. The troops will really charge, and there will be no corks upon the bayonets.

Then, at last, the military doctors for each of these countries will be able to learn their trade and acquire useful experience.

I need not add that an exact reckoning of the killed and wounded will be kept, and subtracted from the victims of the next war.

That, in my opinion, would be one of the most humane measures taken by a civilized nation in years.

And we would have military doctors who are more than rank amateurs.

CHAPTER XLVI

In which we see Captain Cap, then a young man, abuse the science of chemistry to bring trouble into a bourgeois household.

D o you share my opinion? I believe that one should never insult a servant, even mildly.

In exchange for a bit of gold, these people grant us their time and labor: we are even, and need not toss into the balance contemptuous phrases or condescending gestures.

Besides, you may be sure that our domestics will reserve a bit of our own medicine, and, as if by miracle, dose us when the time is right.

Listen then to the excellent joke that a cook of my acquaintance (by this I mean that I was acquainted with the cook, not that she was the cook of an acquaintance of mine), that a cook of my acquaintance, as I was saying, played one day on her stupid and abusive employers.

The cook, whose name was Clémence, was a fine cook, a true professional to her fingertips, and, despite her tender and impetuous nature, perfectly correct in her service.

Her employers were basely born tradespeople, grown wealthy by shady practices, and all the more insolent for it.

The female, especially, was odious.

"Clémence," she never ceased squalling, "Clémence, your Veal Marengo is an utter fiasco."

Mute, Clémence simply shrugged.

"Clémence," the shrew insisted, "your mutton stinks of tallow."

Same reaction on Clémence's part.

One day, it was the salad that the execrable crone went after.

"What's with this salad? Did you dress it with lamp oil?"

And from that moment on, Madame never stopped howling about poor Clémence's salad.

She bought the vinegar herself, as well as the oil: the vinegar from the Duke of Orléans himself, and the oil from Olive in person.

The salad met with no more success.

The fault then was in the proportions: there was too much oil and not enough vinegar.

Or reciprocally.

The old biddy finally decided to make the salad herself.

...At the time, Clémence had as a lover our friend Cap, still young then, and working as an assistant professor of chemistry at an abnormal school.

Informed about his girlfriend's abuse, Cap asked:

"Would you like a good laugh?"

"I'd like nothing better."

"Good. I'll bring the oil and vinegar for you to put ad hoc into the cruets, the next time your monkeys give a big dinner."

The future Captain delivered to his friend a vinegar composed of sulfuric and nitric acid.

The oil was replaced by an excellent glycerine, lightly tinted yellow.

...All of our readers who have spent even two or three years in the serious manufacture of dynamite know that the above mixture forms what is commonly known as nitroglycerine.

When the two liquids are combined brusquely and without precaution, an elevated temperature is produced, followed by one of those explosions that just brings down the curtain (if there's any curtain left).

Everything happened as planned.

Despite all the folderol of the dinner, the lady insisted on dressing the salad herself. The salad bowl was reduced to bits, and the chicory was thrown violently onto the guests.

Unfortunately, the incident was not confined to those few damages.

The dishes and crystal also found it necessary to shatter, as did the table, and the faces and extremities of the ladies and gentlemen.

Meanwhile, in the kitchen were two people who had never laughed so hard.

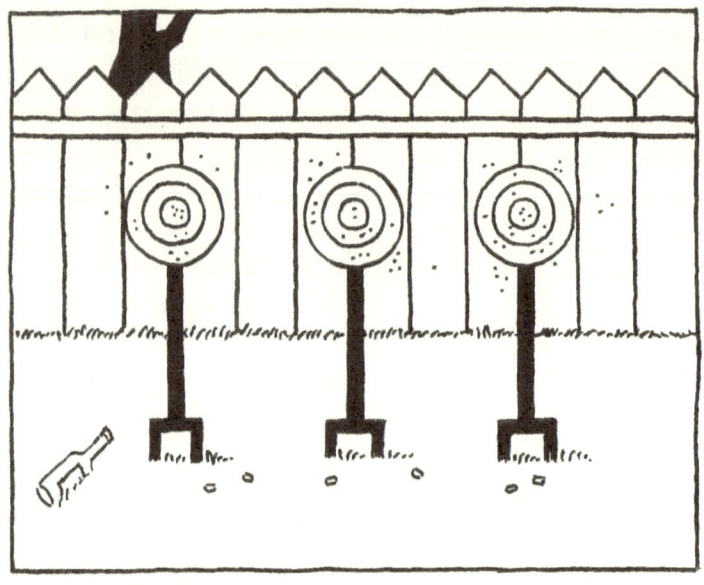

CHAPTER XLVII

The disadvantages of poor pronunciation.

Phil McClure, whom Captain Cap wittily baptizes Phil McCup whenever he overindulges in *stars and stripes*[1], is an amiable and distinguished Bostonian, as are most of the people of Boston.

It was about him that I wrote the following verses, with a rather amusing rhyme, don't you think:

> Phil's waltzing partner's no Medusa:
> She's Mary Webb, of Boston (U. S. A.).[2]

Since his arrival in Paris last spring, this American, upon Cap's recommendation, quickly became my friend.

The French that he spoke was already irreproachable, except for a few words that could have been more correctly pronounced. For example, he sounded the silent "t" in words like *flot* and *pot*.

Once advised, he corrected those minor imperfections, and soon spoke as purely as Le Bargy.

I became quite attached to my friend McClure, a true original, and the soul of spontaneity.

One morning, when I met him on the beach, he proposed a shooting match.

I accepted even more willingly because I knew the ladies

who run the rifle range, lively and pretty young sisters from Montmartre, the elder bearing a name celebrated in the armorial of Parisian gallantry.

McClure, although an excellent shot, was compelled to bow before my crushing superiority; after several rounds, he gave up the fight, and paid our bill into the hands of one of the young ladies, while I complimented the other on the pretty way that her figure was filling out.

"Good-bye, ladies."

"Good-bye, gentlemen. Will we see you this afternoon?"

"Perhaps."

Something was amiss with McClure.

"What's wrong, McClure?" I asked.

"What's wrong is that little Charlotte just made a re-mark that I don't understand."

"What remark?"

"This is what she said, word for word: *How dare you say such a thing! We have enough trouble scraping together a liv-ing, without having to put up with some creep who treats us like dirt!*"

"What did you say to provoke such an enigmatic re-sponse?"

"To pay the 17.50 francs for our match, I gave her a louis, and, as she started to give me the change, I gra-ciously replied (for I'm quite fond of the little creature), 'Keep the rest, miss, for your dowry.'"

"And did you pronounce the word dowry, *dot*, with a silent 't'?"

"Why yes, of course, just as you taught me for *flot*, *pot*, etc."

"That explains it! She thought that you were giving her money for her *dos*."

"I still don't understand."

"*Dos* is a term of Parisian slang for those gentlemen who

gain a detestable revenue from the misconduct of their companions."

"Horrible! Horrible! What must the girl think of me?"

And McClure insisted on returning immediately to the range, to offer his apologies to young Charlotte, along with a pretty ring, for which the little citizen of the eighteenth arrondissement jumped up, threw her arms around his neck, and kissed him with all her heart.

Notes:

1. Into a champagne flute, pour, without stirring, *crème de noyaux,* Maraschino, yellow Chartreuse, Curaçao, and a glass of brandy. Those are the stripes. You'll see the stars when you swig, in one swallow, this spiritous polychromy.

2. Pronounced "United States of America."

Translator's Notes

XXXII: XXXII: Michel Corday's novel about a sanatorium, *Les Embrasés* (*The Feverish*), was published in 1902.

Louis Ternier's authoritative guide, *La Sauvagine en France* (*The Waterfowl of France*), was first published in 1897, and remained in print well into the next century.

XXXIII: Victor Burq did indeed advocate metallotherapy. A "Burquian Commission" was founded to study his claims; Victor Dumontpallier, among others, was a member.

Jules Bernard Luys made many contributions to neuroanatomy and neuropsychiatry. In later years, inspired in part by Burq's research, he devoted himself to the study of hypnosis and hysteria. He fell in with the occultist Gérard Encausse, also known as the Magus Papus; and the two embarked on a series of public demonstrations that ruined Luys's reputation. These included not only the notorious "action of medication at a distance," but storing thoughts in magnetic crowns, visualization of brain emanations, and more. Many of these demonstrations did take place in la Salpêtrière, a psychiatric hospital housed in a former gunpowder factory.

Gaston Méry edited *L'Écho du Merveilleux*, which reported, among other things, Marian apparitions. He is also credited with coining the word "racist," and was himself a prominent anti-Semite.

XXXVI: Verlaine's poem "*Les Chevaux de Bois*" ("Wooden Horses"), from Romances sans paroles, 1874, contains the line "*Tournez, tournez, sans espoir du foin*" ("Turn, turn, without hope of hay").

N. P. Melnikoff received a fair amount of publicity in 1899 for his bacteria motor. It was powered by the gases produced by fermenting yeast.

The Franco-Russian Alliance was drafted in 1892, and ratified in 1894; it called for mutual defense, but implied further economic cooperation.

Pierre Giffard wrote for many newspapers, and organized numerous marathons and bicycle races, as well as the first automobile race (in 1894). His 1899 book, *La Fin du Cheval,* was a humorous defense of the bicycle and automobile.

XXXVII: Joseph Charles Mardrus was best known for his translation of the *Thousand and One Nights.*

XL: For Ferdinand Brunetière, see the note to Chapter XXIX.

XLI: The Drummond Castle left Cape Town for London on May 29, 1896; and sank on June 16 near Molène, off the coast of France. It was a foggy night, with very little visibility. Only three passengers survived; the dead are given by various sources as between 243 and 361.

XLIII: Allais did not invent either Mr. Tourillon or his Porcarine. Their first reporter was apparently Francisque Sarcey, Allais's frequent target, who wrote about them in a column for *Le Matin* on May 12, 1897. In Sarcey's version, Porcarine is the brand name of the lard, not the machine, and can be flavored by introducing herbs into the wounds. Sarcey insisted that Tourillon was not Allais; but did suspect a joke, perhaps on the part of Émile Gautier, a columnist for *Figaro*.

XLV: Pierre Paul Leroy-Beaulieu was indeed a professor of finance at the Free School of Political Science, and held down the chair of political economy at the College of France. He was a champion of colonization. I'm afraid he was also a frequent butt of ridicule for Allais.

XLVI: In the original version, Allais himself was the young chemist, a role perhaps better suited for him than for Cap.

Orléans was once the center of the vinegar industry in France.

XLVII: Charles Le Bargy was an actor in the Comédie-Française.

PART FIVE
Captain Cap's Cocktails

ALABAZAM COCKTAIL: Crushed ice, a few drops of angostura and lemon, a teaspoon of Curaçao. Fill with cognac, strain, add lemon zest, and serve. This is the *Alabazam*.

ALE FLIP: If you are catching a cold, there is nothing like an *ale flip*. This is how to make it. Heat a half glass of pale ale; separately, mix an egg with a tablespoon of sugar, and sprinkle with nutmeg. After beating the mixture well, pour slowly into the beer, stirring vigorously. This drink is like an eggnog with beer.

AMERICAN GROG: Heat one part aged rum and one part water, add sugar, and serve with a slice of lemon stuck with four cloves. Warming and stimulating.

AMERICAN LEMONADE: *American lemonade* is made like ordinary lemonade, with sugar, lemon juice, and seltzer. The only difference is that you add a bit of port.

ANGLER'S COCKTAIL: Are you like me? I adore the *angler's cocktail*. Taste it, and you will see: crushed ice, a few drops of angostura, a teaspoon of orange bitters, another of raspberry syrup; top off with gin, shake, strain, and enjoy.

BRANDY COCKTAIL: Cracked ice, a few drops of angostura, half a spoon of *crème de noyaux*, another of Curaçao, top off with brandy. Shake, strain, add lemon zest, drink.

BRANDY SHANTERALLA: The *brandy shanteralla,* not recommended for the weaker sex, is prepared like this: into cracked ice, pour one tablespoon each of Curaçao, yellow Chartreuse, and anisette; top off with a good cognac.

CHAMPAGNE COBBLER: Fill a large glass with crushed ice, a teaspoon of Curaçao, another of *crème de noyaux,* and finish with that champagne that Saint-Marceaux makes. Stir, add a slice of orange, a slice of lemon, strawberries, and seasonal fruits. Shake, and then, without stirring, drizzle with port. Drink through a straw.

CHAMPAGNE JULEP: Into a large glass, place three or four sprigs of fresh mint, a teaspoon of sugar, and a jigger of cognac. Fill with crushed ice, a jigger of yellow Chartreuse, top off with dry Saint-Marceaux, and stir well. Soak a sprig of mint in lemon and put it in the center of the glass; add seasonal fruits, drizzle with a good rum, and sprinkle with sugar. Drink through a straw.

COFFEE PUNCH: Into a glass of crushed ice, add a half teaspoon of *crème de noyaux*; fill half the glass with Curaçao, add two teaspoons of sugar, a jigger of cognac, another of rum, and one of kirsch. Top off with good black coffee, shake, strain, and drink with a straw.

CORPSE REVIVER: This imaginative recipe is rather difficult to prepare, since the ingredients are of such varying densities. You must pour into a glass, with the aid of a little spoon, taking infinite pains not to mix them, the twelve following liqueurs: grenadine, raspberry, anisette, strawberry, white mint, green Chartreuse, cherry brandy, prunelle, kümmel, guignolet, kirsch, and cognac. Drink in one gulp.

COSMOPOLITAN CLARET PUNCH: In a large glass of crushed ice, add a teaspoon of raspberry syrup, one of Maraschino, one of Curaçao. Add a jigger of brandy, finish with aged bordeaux. A slice of orange, seasonal fruits, a straw.

GIN CLING: To obtain a *gin cling*, heat one part gin and one part water, add sugar and lemon, then pour and drink before it cools.

GIN FLIP: In a glass of cracked ice, add two teaspoons of sugar, a fresh egg yolk, a small amount of *crème de noyaux*, and top off with Old Tom Gin. Shake, strain, pour, and sprinkle with nutmeg. An excellent stimulant when the temperature drops, this *gin flip*.

ICE CREAM SODA: Cap proceeds in this way: into a receptacle filled with ice that he has crushed himself, he adds two jiggers of vanilla liqueur and one of kirsch. He fills the rest with one part milk and one part seltzer. You can vary it to taste by replacing the vanilla with cocoa, or whatever other liqueur you prefer. You can also substitute rum for the kirsch.

ICED CHAMPAGNE: Into a cobbler glass of crushed ice, add a teaspoon of Curaçao, and another of Maraschino, fill with dry Saint-Marceaux, and stir. When ready to serve, add, without stirring, a few drops of a good *crème de vanille*.

IRISH WHISKEY COCKTAIL: The same recipe as the *brandy cocktail*, but replace the brandy with Old Tom Gin.

JOHN COLLINS: An excellent drink for languid mornings, the *John Collins* is prepared in the following fashion: fill a large glass with crushed ice, two teaspoons of sugar, the juice of one lemon, and a jigger of gin. Top off with seltzer or soda, pour, and sip with straws.

LEMON SQUASH: The *lemon squash* is the same as our lemonade: crushed ice, lemon juice, sugar, and seltzer or soda. Stir well, and add a slice of lemon.

MANHATTAN COCKTAIL: An exquisite aperitif, this *Manhattan cocktail*: mix equal parts of whisky and Turin vermouth, add a few drops of angostura and a small spoonful of Curaçao. Crushed ice. Shake, strain, and pour.

MARTINI COCKTAIL: One of the best cocktails when well prepared. Cracked ice, a half tablespoon each of orange bitters, Curaçao, and *crème de noyaux*. Finish with equal parts of gin and Turin vermouth. Shake, strain, and add lemon zest.

MINT JULEP: The *mint julep* is excellent, when you can get fresh mint: crush four sprigs of the plant with a teaspoon of sugar, add a glass of cognac, fill with crushed ice, add a jigger of yellow Chartreuse, top off with water, and stir well. Soak a sprig of mint in lemon juice, and put it in the center of the glass. Add seasonal fruits, and pour over it, without stirring, a dash of rum. Sprinkle with sugar. Drink with a straw.

PICK-ME-UP: The *pick-me-up*, as its name indicates, is recommended as a tonic. To obtain it, put into a silver goblet cracked ice, a tablespoon of lemon juice, another of grenadine, and a third of aged kirsch. Shake, strain, and pour. Fill the glass with Saint-Marceaux and a slice of orange.

ROCKY MOUNTAIN PUNCH: Into a cobbler glass of crushed ice, add two teaspoons of sugar, the juice of half a lemon, half a glass of old rum, a tablespoon of Maraschino, and top off with Saint-Marceaux, a piece of rock candy, and seasonal fruits. Drink with a straw.

STARS AND STRIPES: Into a champagne flute, pour, without stirring, crème de noyaux, Maraschino, yellow Chartreuse, Curaçao, and a glass of brandy.

THUNDER: A great stimulant, the *thunder:* cracked ice, a half teaspoon of sugar, a whole fresh egg, and a jigger of old cognac. Add a generous pinch of cayenne pepper. Beat, strain, and drink.

WHISKEY COCKTAIL: Put into your cocktail shaker a few pieces of ice, a few drops of angostura, a small amount of Curaçao and *crème de noyaux*, and complete with scotch. Shake, strain, and pour. When the cocktail is served, cut a lemon rind carefully into thin strips, bruise them to release the oil, and add them to your glass.

WHISKEY STONE FENCE: The *whiskey stone fence* is simply an excellent cider, sweetened and beaten, into which you pour a glass of Irish or Scotch whiskey. You can also replace these spirits with calvados.

PART SIX
8 Uncollected Cap Tales

THE CHAMELEON CHILD
by Captain Cap

The boy is weak, and getting thinner.
His brutal father, out of spite,
Delivers beatings for his dinner,
And little Gustave's pale and white.

He tries to act with due discretion,
But stumbles on a pail instead.
And at his father's fierce expression,
Poor little Gustave's poppy-red.

His vicious father often chooses
A blow as something fun to do.
The boy is covered now with bruises,
And little Gustave's black and blue.

Poor child! At last his life has ended:
A bud the sun had never seen.
Within his tomb he lies distended,
And little Gustave's turning green.

LOUDER AND LOUDER

This morning, I met a man, still young, who pays me 600 francs a year just to keep his name out of the papers, but whom we will nevertheless designate by the sobriquet of *Captain Cap*.

Captain Cap is a curious soul, who seems to incarnate a penchant for meteorology, a thorough knowledge of marine matters, and an aptitude for the racetrack (not to mention a keen appetite for cosmopolitan drinks).

Having traveled widely, Captain Cap has retained a great deal, from insights into Australian esthetics to the jig tunes of San Francisco.

Captain Cap is what is known as *somebody*.

Since I met him, I cannot recall spending five minutes in his company without some new little surprise, sometimes trivial, but always something (and without the slightest change in his expression, besides).

So, this morning, we found ourselves on the terrace of a cafe on the Champs-Elysées (we often go to cafes, Captain Cap and I).

No waiter to serve us.

Cap pulls a ten centime piece from his pocket, and strikes the marble table with some violence.

The summons is in vain.

Calmly, Cap replaces the humble copper knocker with a five franc coin. And he raps, and he raps, and he raps.

The unsettling torpor of the cafe does not awaken by one iota.

Then, our bold Captain Cap, who wants the last word—as well as a drink, finally!—extracts from his billfold a thousand franc note, with which he furiously hammers the table.

It is only at this notification that the waiter decides to place himself at our service.

FRESH EGGS WITH CAPTAIN CAP

It has apparently been quite a while since I reported the conversation of my fine friend, the intrepid navigator Captain Cap.

A neglect that is easily remedied; for yesterday, I spent with him two of the most agreeable hours of my existence.

When I tell you that our meeting took place in an English bar, near the Opera House, I hope that you will not be surprised.

"Well, my excellent Cap!"

"Good day, my child! Still doing well?"

"Well enough, thanks, and you too, I hope?"

"Not too badly... I purged myself this morning, and in such an unusual way!"

"Oh, bah!"

"Yes, just imagine that yesterday I bought a bottle of Hunyadi-Janos, which I prepared to consume, this morning... But let me laugh a bit about it, won't you?"

"I was going to encourage you."

"The curtains of my room being hermetically closed, I took the wrong bottle, and instead of the magnesia water, swallowed an entire flask of Old Tom Gin. What do you say to that?"

"I say, Cap, that you hold the record for distraction. And you didn't see your error in time?"

"I told you: the curtains of my room were tightly sealed!"

"That explains it. So then, you didn't purge yourself?"

"I beg your pardon! In that kind of operation, imagination is all. Drink a glass of Curaçao, convinced that it's ipecac, and see if you don't vomit up your guts and intestines!"

"That may well be..."

"Certainly!... Such was my case. Believing that I had swallowed the Hunyadi-Janos, I passed through all the stratagems of the sport... And I needed it badly, I assure you."

"Please, Cap, no details!"

At that moment, into the bar walked one of Cap's friends, who will play no part in the rest of our story, but whose words deserve to be reported.

He addressed the proprietor:

"Of course, madam, I cannot claim to be perfect, and do not present myself as such. Like all of humanity, I have my little faults; but there is one thing that none can take from me: and that is that I am damnably thirsty. Please, madam, bring me a large glass of ginger-beer."

Captain Cap shrugged imperceptibly, and returned to our conversation.

"The strangest thing is that my pseudo-purgative has terribly upset my stomach. I believe I'll have a *port wine egg flip*. And you too, I suppose?"

"Without a doubt."

"Are you looking at my hat? Isn't it wonderful! It's a new design that I'm launching with good old Barjau.[1] And practical? You have no idea!"

Port wine egg flip is a comforting cocktail which contains port wine and egg yolk.

While the waiter beat the egg yolk, an idea reoccurred to Cap.

"Do you know what class of tradesmen holds the record for stupidity?"

"I can't think of it."

"Egg dealers, my friend. You have no idea what idiots egg dealers are."

"Well, that's funny. I never noticed."

"Perhaps you were never in the egg business?"

"I rack my memory in vain; I find no connection to the industry."

"Ah, yes! They're idiots, those egg dealers! My God, what idiots they are!"

"As bad as that?"

"Oh, even worse!... Are you unaware that fresh eggs command a higher price than the eggs of yesteryear?"

"I do know that."

"It is obvious that an egg laid this morning will cost more than one elaborated during the Crimean War."

---

1. Not content with being named Alfred, Barjau is also the best hatter in Paris, near the Saint-Lazare station (5 Havre Street).

"Hooray for Russia!"

"So then, why do those imbeciles wait for their eggs to be stale before selling them? Why? I ask you: why?"

"Very true, in fact!"

"Therefore, I have founded the *General Society for Fresh Eggs of the Seine*. We will buy great tracts of land, where we will raise millions of fowl... No sooner has an egg left the chicken's ass... It doesn't offend you, I hope, if I use this vulgar term?"

"Yes, a bit, but I'll get used to it."

"No sooner, I say, has an egg left the chicken's ass, then we throw it upon the market."

"Not too hard, though, or you'll break it."

"Since the egg is fresh, we get a high price for it, and, at the same time, save considerably on storage. What do you say to that?"

"I say, my dear Cap, that if you, instead of Carnot, sat upon the throne of France, business would work quite differently than it works now."

And because the *egg flip* had left an unpleasant aftertaste, we ordered a good glass of *Irish whiskey*.

GOVERNMENT REGULATION

The welcome that Captain Cap had reserved for me was completely devoid of—how shall I put it?—expansiveness. (You may attribute this fact to a recent misunderstanding.)

But Cap's soul is a great soul, and Cap, upon seeing my dejected expression, my visible chagrin, could not keep his welcome at such a chilly temperature.

On the contrary, even; I saw him suddenly leap onto the platform of cordiality.

"What will you have, Allais?"

"I was about to ask you, Captain."

"A wine spritzer for me."

"And for me, sugar water with orange blossom."

"Go easy on the orange blossom; it's quite strong in this place... Be careful!"

And Cap, after a brief silence:

"Do you remember, my dear Alphonse, a conversation that we had recently concerning eggs?"

"Perfectly!... Kippered herring eggs, wasn't it, with which Casimir Périer amused himself by incubating with stuffed ostriches?"

"No, not those. I refer to chicken eggs."

"Chicken eggs?"

"Yes, chicken eggs. Your eyes have opened wide... Are you unaware that chickens are oviparous?"

"No, Cap. I was initiated into that detail at an early age."

"Do you not remember that one day I was admiring (admiring in the Latin sense of the word: *mirari, to be astonished*), I was admiring that egg dealers were idiots not to sell their fresh eggs immediately, at a good price, instead of waiting—as they do—until those same eggs have lost their freshness, and with it their value?"

"I remember, Cap."

"That's fortunate... Do you know what happened to one of my friends, with this system?"

"I burn to know."

"My friend, last night, enters a market. He asks for a fresh egg, *the freshest egg that they have,* to consume before retiring."

"An excellent habit."

"My friend returns home... With one sharp blow of the knife, he cracks the shell, and from this shell suddenly emerges a little chick. Furious at being bothered at such an hour, the young galliform jumps up to my friend's eyes and pecks out both of them."

"Now there's an unusual occurrence!"

"Unusual or not, such an adventure should never happen in a government elected by universal franchise."

"But what is the solution?"

"It has been discovered! One of my friends..."

"The one whose eyes were pecked out?"

"No, another one... an aviculturalist near Valence, whose card this is: Baldek-Hatzar, from Vélau (Drôme), has solved the problem. My God, it's quite simple!"

"Speak freely, Cap."

"Here it is. The government will assume a monopoly on eggs, as it has already for tobacco and matches. Every hen exercising her industry on the territory of the French republic will be equipped, on her posterior orifice, with a machine to register, count, and date each egg. The machine, which is essentially quite simple, is composed of a clock that gives the time and date, an ink roller, and a date stamp. The whole thing weighs 68 grams and 99 centigrams."

"Marvelous, Cap, marvelous!"

"So, no more trickery, no more fraud, no more unexpected chicks! The tests that have been made have been entirely successful. My friend, the Turk Baldek-Hatzar, wrote to the Minister of Agriculture, and to the Minister of Finance. Those gentlemen have not bothered to respond. Ah, what a lovely thing it is, your Europe!"

"You're telling me!"

And Cap ordered two cups of lime-blossom tea, which we gaily quaffed before parting.

THE MAIN ATTRACTION AT THE 1900 EXPOSITION

"Tell me, Captain, have you kept up with all of the different proposals for the 1900 Exposition?"

"I've known about them for some time. All of them betray a sad paucity of imagination, except that of my friend Otto, which consists of an enormous swing which would carry entire families between the Trocadéro and the Military Academy. Now that's no banal idea!"

"Indeed!... And will you, Captain, take part in this peaceful tournament?"

"I plan to... At the moment, I have two projects, one large and one small."

"The small one first?"

"Oh, it's nothing. A new musical tire."

"Well, well!"

"Yes, a series of small accordions that I install inside a tire, and which make a rather entertaining music, I must say!"

"But does it always play the same tune?"

"Not at all! By means of an ingenious mechanism, and thanks to a simple switch, the cyclist can change the tune at will."

"My congratulations, Captain, for such a simple and charming idea. Those tires will be far more cheerful than the Formalat tire, which I find a bit severe."

Usually, Captain Cap has no taste for pleasantries based solely on a play on words. This time, however, he did not flinch, and even added:

"I always insist on the Pericles. It's the prince of tires."

Having smiled, as was customary, at our respective pleasantries, we returned to more austere subjects.

"And your large idea, Cap?"

"Well, then!"

I had to insist.

"My large idea, and yes, you're right, it is a large idea, is, quite simply, the solution to aerial navigation."

"A dirigible?"

"Poor child!"

"An aerostat, with motors turning the wings?"

"Idiot!"

"Be polite, Captain!"

"Idiot, I say!... Have you ever seen swarms of grasshoppers?"

"Never."

"Well, my apparatus is a swarm of grasshoppers, ten million grass-hoppers, which I will enclose in an immense gauze bag (green gauze, of course, so as not to tire my grasshoppers' eyes).

"A wise precaution!"

"The gauze bag is supported by a gigantic bamboo frame, on which Comiot is currently working."

"An excellent firm, that Comiot!"

"And there will be not only grasshoppers in my bag, but also fleas, because fleas have the singular property of greatly stimulating the activity of grasshoppers. Did you know that?"

"I was unaware of that detail."

"Each grasshopper, without even exerting itself, represents a little more than a gram of ascensional force. Ten million grasshoppers represents a usable force of ten million kilos, eh?"

"Amazing!... But one simple objection, Captain?"

"Go ahead."

"How will you steer this little population, when you want to go north, and the grasshoppers show a pronounced preference for the south?"

"Nothing simpler! Grasshoppers detest carbon disulfide. So, by the ad hoc use of a vaporizer, I poison the atmosphere in the opposite direction from the one I desire. Do I want to head east? I spray the stink on the west side of the sack, and you should see those little wings go!"

"And when you want to stop?"

"Belts, under my control, constrict the gauze, and gradually paralyze the efforts of my insects."

"Congratulations, Captain. Your idea is a brilliant one."

"Ah! Well, you see, it's because I never went to the Polytechnic!"

A USE FOR THE EIFFEL TOWER IN 1900

At the risk of causing great sorrow to Maurice Barrès, the authorities seem inclined to mount a Universal Exposition in 1900.

It will be news to nobody when I add that those magnificent jousts between international industries will be enacted in the areas of the Champ de Mars, Trocadéro, and the Champs-Elysées.

They will even go so far as to demolish—oh weep, my eyes!—that marvel of construction and grace that is the Palace of Industry.

The question of dismantling the Eiffel Tower was momentarily debated in high places. (Perhaps those high places were nothing but the third platform of said tower.)

The discussion was lengthy, it appears.

Finally, upon the observation of a judicious soul that, the committee of the Legion of Honor having bestowed a rosette upon Mr. Eiffel, they might very well preserve his tower, it was decided that they would not yet unrivet the metallic edifice.

Upon learning of this resolution, my friend Captain Cap smiled under his long mustache, drained in one gulp the goblet at hand, and said:

"I have an idea."

"The contrary would astound me, Cap!"

"An idea to find a use for that stupid tower, which was, in 1889, a useful industrial demonstration, but which has now become perfectly pointless."

"And besides, we've seen enough of it, that Eiffel Tower!"

"We've seen enough of it!... Let us keep it, then, but give it a different look."

"What if we put it upside down, with its top on the bottom, and its feet in the air?"

"Exactly what I was thinking. But my idea does not end there."

"Your idea, Cap, could never end there! Like time, like space, it knows no bounds!"

"Thank you, my boy!... Therefore, we will set the Eiffel Tower upside down, with its top on the bottom, and its paws in the air. Then, we will envelop it in a coat of magnificent, decorative, and perfectly impermeable porcelain."

"Bravo, Cap!... And then?"

"And then, when I have made it absolutely watertight, I will install taps on the bottom and fill it with water."

"With water, Captain? Horrors!"

"Yes, with water... Of course, before the operation, I will have rid the tower of all wooden elements, and, in general, of all organic material which might pollute my water. Can you guess now?"

"I guess, or think that I can guess, that you will display for the admiration of the public a sumptuous quadrangular goblet 300 meters high."

"A goblet filled with what?"

"A goblet filled with water."

"What kind of water?"

"I understand!... Ferruginous water. Ah, Cap, you are a genius!"

"Yes, ferruginous water, freely available to all of our anemic contemporaries. After a few years, the entire mass of iron, dissolved bit by bit in rainwater, will have passed into the organisms of the people of Paris, bringing them vigor and health."

"What if we used gin instead of water, Cap, good old gin?"

The Captain answered me severely:

"The taste of gin does not go well with the taste of iron."

A REVOLUTION IN SAILING

A quantity of readers write me every day, to complain about the silence in which I have let fall the adventures and accomplishments of Captain Cap.

Captain Cap is no longer my friend, and, henceforth, that navigator's name shall not issue from my pen.

I would have preferred not to broach this sorry affair in public, but given that Cap is probably behind bars by now, there is no longer any indiscretion in revealing one of the most shameful turpitudes of the century, and one with which the press will busy itself tomorrow.

Simply put, Captain Cap sold to Germany the plans for the mobilization, in time of war, of the laundry-boats on the Seine.

The consequences of this treasonous act will escape nobody: it means the Seine delivered to the enemy, from Rouen to Bourgogne; it means Paris at the mercy of attack.

How was Cap able to procure the mobilization plans? Nothing simpler.

Without being an official member of the commission for the fortification of laundry-boats, the Captain has often been called as a consultant, for he is one of the best informed men in the world on this important question.

Therefore, it was very easy for him to copy certain documents kept secret from the rest of the world.

We can lose ourselves in conjecture on the motives that persuaded our former friend to commit such a vile act.

It is not the need for money, the Captain being quite wealthy, and still earning enormous sums in the traffic of ivory and mouse tails.

What is it then?

Could it be his fierce anti-Europeanism that goaded him into provoking an even greater rift between these two great nations of his detested Europe?

Whatever it was, after serious inquiry, the traitor's guilt has been established, and Cap must have been arrested this morning.

I have known of this sordid business for over a year, but it revolted me to have to denounce such an old comrade, and I preferred to let matters follow their natural course.

You can say what you like, but I consider the downfall of such a brilliant personality sad news indeed.

His last invention was one of those that astonish the world, and that herald a new era in world history in general, and in that of sailing in particular.

While all branches of industry have made great progress over the last thousand years, sailing has remained stationary.

The structure of ships has certainly been improved, and the arrangement of sails perfected, etc., etc., but no really new idea has revolutionized seamanship.

The honor of that decisive step was reserved for Cap.

And yet how simple, really, was his idea!

The Captain replaces the sails with a series of windmills, whose combined captured force moves a powerful propellor.

Wind used as a motor, rather than as a propulsive force, enjoys three and a half times as much power (others have done the calculation before me).

With a strong breeze, Captain Cap's new craft can attain twenty-seven knots, which, you must admit, constitutes a pretty bit of speed for a simple windjammer.

Let me add that the ship, with all of its windmills, offers an infinitely more picturesque spectacle than one powered by sails, or even by steam.

Therein lies the future.

How unfortunate that such a marvelous inventor is also a vicious criminal!

GOOD NEWS FOR MOTHERS

I have good news to impart to those of my readers who take an interest in my little personal affairs: the cold air that chilled the radiator of our relations, between Captain Cap and me, has recently returned to a balmier phase.

We are friends, the intrepid navigator and I, like in the good old days.

You may remember the cause of this resentment: the accusations that Cap had delivered to the enemy the mobilization plans for our laundry-boats in time of war.

It appears that it was nothing but old wives' tales, and baseless farragoes from the residents of Arago Boulevard (naturally).

Upon the testimony of one of Cap's friends, an unimpeachably honorable character, and, what is more, almoner of the Eiffel Tower, my last suspicions evaporated, and my hand, of its own accord, sought that of my old friend.

...It would take a huge volume, as fat as a phone book, just to summarize the Captain's accomplishments in this past year.

The industry of the man, his brilliance, and his elevated humanity, would give vertigo to the best trained alpinist.

Such men are the honor of our globe.

Would anyone have suspected, for example, that Captain Cap has just given France a new weapon that will render her invincible, at a time when the whole world in in league against her?

Not to mention that France will emerge victorious from the greatest conflict without spilling a single drop of blood, either from our ranks or those of the enemy!

If you refuse to call that a result, my little friends, you are damnably difficult, and I have but one reply:

Do better, clever dicks!

And how simple Cap's plan is, how easy to realize, and how inexpensive!

Here is the idea in a nutshell:

Captain Cap does away with the infantry, the cavalry, and the engineers, and keeps only the artillery.

Except that the shells, instead of being loaded with melinite and other homicidal materials, are filled with itching powder.

You read that correctly: *itching powder.*

Hold your laughter, young ninnies!

One need not have passed through the Polytechnic School, or other nurseries for blockheads, to understand fully the properties of itching powder.

Can you picture it?

An entire regiment suddenly enveloped in opaque clouds of this intolerable and irritating substance!

In order to scratch themselves, the most valiant warriors drop sabers and rifles, forget to load cannons, and, above all, cannot aim them.

Horsemen drop the reins of their steeds.

In brief, general confusion.

Meanwhile, what do we, the brave little French soldiers, do during this time?

We pounce upon all of those ridiculous individuals, load them with chains, and march the whole jolly crew off into captivity, where we burden them with repugnant tasks, until the enemy nations pay us millions upon millions, as if it were raining money.

Translator's Notes

"The Chameleon Child" appeared in an 1894 anthology by the Chat Noir, *Les Gaietés du Chat Noir*. Although attributed to Captain Cap, it could have been written by Allais, or, for that matter, any of the Captain's admirers, who were legion.

"Louder and Louder" appeared in Allais's 1893 collection, *Le Parapluie de l'Escouade*.

"Fresh Eggs with Captain Cap" first appeared in Allais's column for *Le Journal*, November 20, 1893; and was reprinted in *Rose et Vert-Pomme* (1894).

Hunyadi-Janos Bitterquelle was a popular mineral water, bottled in Ofen, Hungary, and prized for its laxative properties.

I hope that Allais got a nice hat from Barjau for the plug.

Carnot was, at the time, President of France.

"Government Regulation" is from *Le Journal*, May 20, 1894; it was reprinted in *2 + 2 = 5* (1895).

Casimir Périer became President in 1894, after Carnot's assassination.

"The Main Attraction at the 1900 Exposition" is from *Le Journal*, November 6, 1894; it was reprinted in *2 + 2 = 5*.

Comiot manufactured bicycles and motorcycles (see Chapter XXI).

The Polytechnic School, in Palaiseau, near Paris, is a prestigious military engineering school.

"A Use for the Eiffel Tower in 1900" is from *Le Journal*, January 20, 1896; it was reprinted in *Le Bec en l'air* (1897).

Maurice Barrès opposed the Exposition in articles in *Figaro*, claiming that it would cost the provinces, but only benefit Paris. Once it opened, he memorably denounced it as "lemonade and prostitution."

"A Revolution in Sailing" is from *Le Journal*, November 26, 1896; it was reprinted in *Amours, délices, et orgues* (1898).

"Good News for Mothers" is from *Le Journal*, April 28, 1897.

CAPPENDIX

The only known photo of Captain Cap, Albert Caperon, distributed during his 1893 campaign.

ÉLECTIONS LÉGISLATIVES DU 20 AOUT 1893

IXe Arrondissement ~ 2me Circonscription

COMITÉ ANTI-EUROPÉEN ET ANTI-BUREAUCRATE

CITOYENS,

Saint-Just a dit: "Vous avez renversé l'Aristocratie, mais vous avez créé la **BUREAUCRATIE**!"
Il y a cent ans de cela et aujourd'hui la **BUREAUCRATIE** est plus que jamais toute puissante.
Elle a tout englobé, tout absorbé, tout envahi!
C'est elle qui étouffe les génies et tue les grandes idées: elle est la plaie européenne et l'entrave à tout progrès!
Jusqu'ici, aucun des candidats qui se sont présentés n'a paru soupçonner l'existence de ce Monstre formidable accroupi aux portes de la Civilisation!
Cette pieuvre aux 100,000 tentacules, nul n'a osé l'attaquer.

Or, un homme s'est levé:

Le CAPTAIN CAP

Et c'est dans le Quartier St Georges qu'il a voulu être le St Georges de ce Dragon!
Un homme s'est levé, Citoyens, et cet homme a regardé autour de lui!
Son regard a été obscurci par des nuages de sandaraque.
Autour de lui il n'a vu que **PAPERASSES, IGNORANCE, INCURIE** et **ROUTINE**.
PLUS DE RONDS DE CUIR! s'est-il écrié. Assez longtemps nous avons obéi aux **MANCHES DE LUSTRINE**.
Les temps sont venus de renverser cette **BASTILLE DE CARTONS VERTS**!
Alors, sans hésiter, à notre demande, il a tout quitté, son bord et ses chères études, pour saisir **LA BARRE DU PAQUEBOT DE NOS REVENDICATIONS**!
Tout le monde sur le pont! a-t-il commandé, et à l'abordage de la **GALÈRE BUREAUCRATIQUE**!
Citoyens, cet homme est le vôtre!
Nous sommes sûrs de lui comme de nous mêmes: nous avons son passé pour garantie.
Astronome distingué, chimiste, baleinier, ingénieur, pêcheur de perles, trappeur, négociant et surtout, vaillant marin, il a au cours de ses incursions dans les différentes parties du globe acquis une expérience incontestable.
Ayant gardé au cœur l'amour vivace de la terre natale, il a conçu pour les institutions vermoulues de sa patrie une haine implacable.
Au Far-West le **CAPTAIN CAP** a combattu les Arapahoes. Il les a vaincus, il a scalpé leur chef!
Il va s'attaquer maintenant à ceux que dans son langage imagé il appelle "**LES SAUVAGES BLANCS, LES PLUS DANGEREUX DE TOUS**!"
Telles sont, Citoyens, les grandes lignes de notre programme.
Le Captain, comme il vous l'a dit est de plus nettement **ANTI-EUROPEEN**.
L'expression d'une idée aussi noble et aussi généreuse se passe de commentaires.

Donc, Citoyens, aux urnes et pas d'abstentions!

Votons pour ALBERT CAPERON

DIT LE

CAPTAIN CAP

LE COMITÉ:

Maurice O'Reilly, Paul Frény, Alphonse Allais, Raoul Ponchon, George Auriol, Léon Gandillot, Howard Symonds, Georges Courteline, Emile Goudeau, Armand Berthez, Raphael Shoomard, Jean Prairial, Narcisse Lebeau, Georges Gatget, Paul Thomaschet junior, Lacault, A. Bert, Jules Jouy, Gerault "du Cantal,, Pol Pharaon, Poulain, Edouard Million, J. Paulet, Darcey, Ribeyrolles, Petit, Alfred-Amand Montel, Jehan Sarrazin, Georges Gaybeslile, Thébaut, Louis Déan de Polonceau, Mateu, Bruyas, Armand Guilmot, F. Huguenet, Saint Just Maurice Minart, Edmond Prouillet, Paul Robert, Charles Quinel, docteur Vivier, docteur de Martilly, docteur Boulanger, Chevreux, ingénieur.
Les deux Mousis, les deux Stevens, les deux Berthier, les deux Prévost, les deux Pornin.

Vu le Candidat ALBERT CAPÉRON dit CAPTAIN CAP

A campaign poster for Captain Cap.

Allais in performance, drawn by Maurice Henry.

Cover illustration by Doug Skinner for volume one of the limited edition of *Captain Cap* published in the *Absurdist Texts & Documents* series.

Allais at his desk, in 1890.

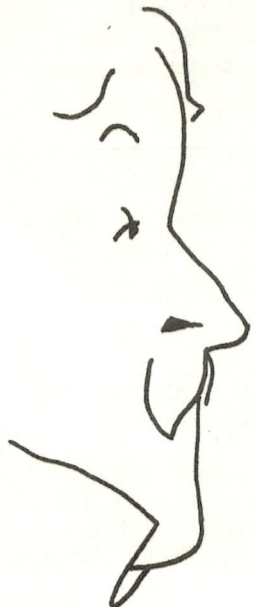

Allais, as sketched by Sacha Guitry.

2ᵉ ANNÉE. — Nᵒ 2.   **Prix : 10 centimes**   Le 28 Janvier 1880

L'HYDROPATHE

Rédacteur en chef : ÉMILE GOUDEAU

Directeur : **Paul VIVIEN.** — *Administrateur :* **Maurice PETIT.** — *Secrétaire de la Rédaction :* **Émile COHL.**

ADMINISTRATION — RÉDACTION	ABONNEMENTS	BUREAUX DE VENTE
19, rue du Sommerard, 19	Paris.................... 3 fr. » Province et étranger...... 3 fr. 50	**13, rue Mouge et 32, rue d'Angoulême.**

Allais as pharmacist, portrayed by Cabriol (Georges Lorin) on the cover of *L'Hydropathe*, January 25, 1880.

Major Heitner, Allais, and Cap, caricatured by Jean Veber for
Le Journal, January 6, 1896.

Allais as depicted by Guirand de Scévola.

One of the last photos of Allais.

ABOUT THE AUTHOR

Alphonse Allais (1854-1905) was a peerless French humorist, celebrated posthumously by the Surrealists for his elegant style and disturbing imagination. In addition to composing absurdist texts for newspapers such as *Le Chat Noir* and *Le Journal*, he experimented with holorhymes, invented conceptual art, and created the earliest known example of a silent musical composition: *Funeral March for the Obsequies of a Deaf Man* (1884). Truly ahead of his time (as well as ours), Allais is needed now more than ever. His mischievous work remains fresh, funny, and always surprising.

ABOUT THE TRANSLATOR

Doug Skinner has written numerous scores for theater and dance, particularly for actor/clown Bill Irwin (*The Regard of Flight*). His articles, cartoons, and translations have appeared in *The Fortean Times, Fate, The Anomalist, Nickelodeon, Weirdo, Black Scat Review,* and other periodicals. His translation of Giovanni Battista Nazari's alchemical dream vision, *Three Dreams,* was published by Magnum Opus Hermetic Sourceworks in 2002. His translation of Isidore Isou's *Considerations on the Death and Burial of Tristan Tzara* is #8 in the *Absurdist Texts & Documents* series published by Black Scat.

Sublime Art & Literature from
Black Scat Books

Allais, Alphonse. MASKS
Allais, Alphonse. HOW I BECAME AN IDIOT BY FRANCISQUE SARCEY
Translated from the French by Doug Skinner
Allais, Alphonse. CAPTAIN CAP: HIS ADVENTURES, HIS IDEAS, HIS DRINKS
Translated from the French by Doug Skinner
Anonymous. ADVENTURES IN 'PATAPHYSICS
Arias-Misson, Alain. THE MAN WHO WALKED ON AIR
& OTHER TALES OF INNOCENCE
Arias-Misson, Alain. TINTIN MEETS THE DRAGON QUEEN
in THE RETURN OF THE MAYA TO MANHATTAN
Bacon, G. Mackenzie. WASTED ENERGIES, BAFFLED THOUGHTS:
ON THE WRITING OF THE INSANE
Balzac, Honoré de. WAITING FOR GODEAU
Translated from the French by Mark Axelrod
Bianchessi, Peppo. CONTEMPORARY ART FOR RICH KIDS
Bracciolini, Poggio. THE FACETIAE EROTICA OF POGGIO
Cami, Pierre Henri. A CAMI SAMPLER
Translated from the French by John Crombie
Carolino, Pedro. COLD IN THE BRAIN. Annotated by Paul Forristal
Conquest, Norman. THE NEGLECTED WORKS OF NORMAN CONQUEST
Conquest, Norman. SNOWDROP IN AFRICA
Debut, Farewell. THE TWO LOVES OF NUNNY
Debut, Farewell. BLINK: VISUAL ANTIPHONIES
Forsythe, Ryan. IF YOU DON'T READ THIS THE TERRORISTS WILL WIN
Gerdes, Eckhard. 'S A BIRD
Hibbard, Cecil Sears. THE OTHER SIDE: THE SHOCKING TRUTH BEHIND
100 CLASSIC PAINTINGS
Isou, Isidore. CONSIDERATIONS ON THE DEATH AND BURIAL
OF TRISTAN TZARA. Translated from the French by Doug Skinner
Kasper, M. KIRGHIZ STEPPES: ACCUMULATED VERBO-VISUALS
Kostelanetz, Richard. THE WORKS & LIFE OF KOSTY RICHARDS:
AN AMERICAN CAREER
Leigh, Michael. THE BEST OF THE CHRISTMAS CATALOGUES
Leigh, Michael & Conquest, Norman. IT'S FUN TO BE RICH IN AMERICA
Memi, Samantha. KATE MOSS & OTHER HEROINES
Mori, Monika. SHATTERED RAINBOW
Mori, Monika. MOO NUDES
Nations, Opal Louis. THE COMPLETE UNABRIDGED LEXICON
Nations, Opal Louis. EMBRYO WORLD & OTHERS STRIPPED BARE
Nickle, John. NICKLE NOIR: THE ART OF JOHN NICKLE
Pell, Derek. THE WONDERFUL WIZARD OF SADE
Pell, Derek. DOKTOR BEY'S SUICIDE GUIDEBOOK
Skinner, Doug. THE UNKNOWN ADJECTIVE & OTHER STORIES
Southern, Terry. HOT HEART OF BOAR & OTHER TASTES
Various. OULIPO PORNOBONGO: ANTHOLOGY OF EROTIC WORDPLAY
Various. OULIPO PORNOBONGO 2
Whalen, Tom. DOLL WITH CHILI PEPPER
Whalen, Tom. HOTEL ORTOLAN. With photographs by Michel Varisco

BlackScatBooks.com